**The Dressage Guide To Series**
"Circles and Corners"

MW00946554

Design and cover art by Krystal Kelly.

Disclaimer: This publication is designed to provide accurate and authoritative information regarding the subject matter covered. The author makes no guarantees to the results you'll achieve by reading this book. Horse riding requires risk and hard work. The results and client case studies presented in this book represent results achieved working directly with the author. Your results may vary when undertaking any new training plan or horse riding strategy.

To the team who lives The International Equestrian daily and serves our clients with all your heart and soul, thank you.

**"Your desire for something is not an indicator of your seriousness. It's the actions you take."**
-Grant Cardone

# Dressage Square

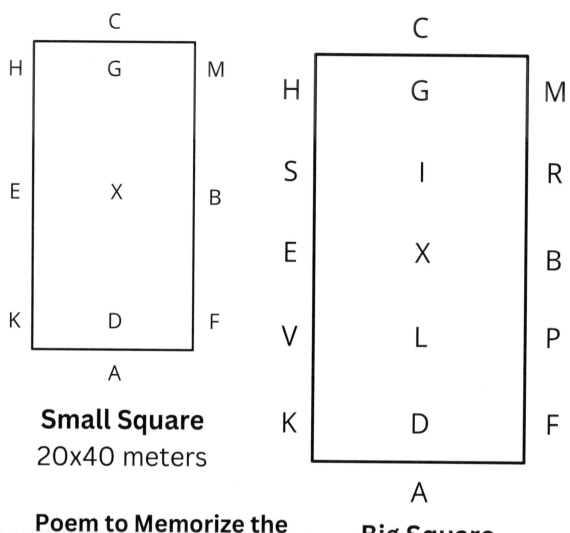

**Small Square**
20x40 meters

**Big Square**
20x60 meters

**Poem to Memorize the Centerline Letters:**
**D**ressage **L**ife **I**s **G**ood

**Poem to Memorize the Order of the Letters:**
**A**ll **K**ing **V**ictor **E**dward's **S**how **H**orses' **C**an **M**ake **R**eally **B**ig **P**retty **F**ences

# Dressage Poem

Can

Horses     Good     Make

Show     Is     Really

Edward's     X     Big

Victor     Life     Pretty

King     Dressage     Fences

All

# THE HORSE TRAINING SCALE

AN EASY BREAKDOWN OF THE HOW THE TRAINING SCALE WORKS TO MOVE YOUR HORSE UP IN LEVELS. (FOR ALL DISCIPLINES!)

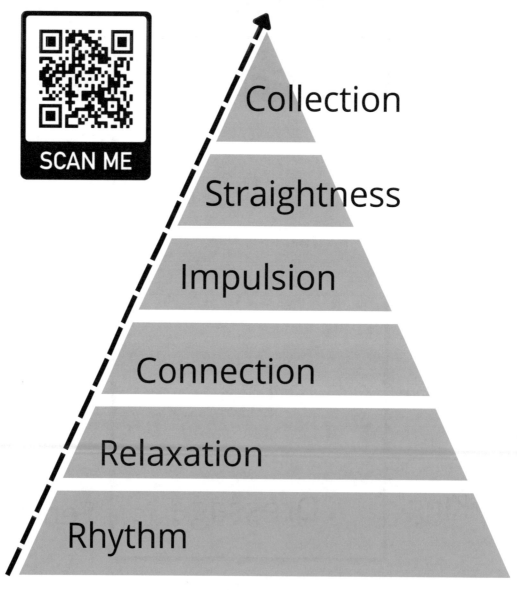

SCAN ME

Collection

Straightness

Impulsion

Connection

Relaxation

Rhythm

# The International Equestrian

### Achieving your riding goals *is our business.*

## WELCOME TO THE INTERNATIONAL EQUESTRIAN TRIBE!

Thank you for purchasing this workbook. As a thank you for your support we want to give you access to this special bonus to help support you on your quest. All you have to do to access your bonus coaching support is to join our facebook group and share your "homework" inside our group.

**https://www.facebook.com/groups/theinternationalequestrian**

**Step 1:** Join our Facebook Group
**Step 2:** Turn in your riding videos & #homework
**Step 3:** Get feedback from a real FEI Coach!

## SCAN ME

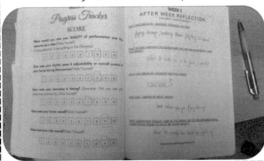

"Hohooo I am controlling my horse s speed! BIG DISCOVERY ( after finishing W5 of sticky butt) when I RIDE ACTIVELY all the way to the fence my spicy mare follows MY RHYTHM and doesnt speed up!!!! I can't believe it how come I didn't figure it out myself??? Thank you Krystal Kelly !!!"
- Kristýna from Czech Republic

SCAN ME

🎓 Claim your 🎓
# $500 Scholarship

As a thank you for getting my book... I'd like to extend you a very special invitation for a select few lucky riders to join me for our "Sticky Butt Bootcamp" Coaching. These lucky riders will recieve a $500 scholarship to apply to their tuition fees.

All you have to do is visit our website. If we have openings please use this special code: **stickybuttersunite500** at checkout to enroll and save **$500 on your tuition fees.**

*Limited availability: If there are no openings you can get on our waitlist by emailing us at: info@theinternationalequestrian.com

# HOW THIS BOOK IS DIFFERENT

I am a professional show jumper. *GASP!*

In fact, I am currently the ONLY FEI level II Show Jumping Coach from the USA, Canada, the UK, Australia (basically the only one from an English-speaking country.)

Right now 50% of the dressage riders reading this book either A) closed the book immediately and will never open this book again B) thought to themselves "why should I listen to you? You don't know anything about dressage!"

And to that I say, "I am the ONLY person qualified to teach you what I am about to teach you inside this book." (Literally. The only person with this qualification and one of the youngest to achieve it since I got my FEI II when I was 25 years old in Greece. All 3 of my FEI II coaches I'd trained with personally had gotten the same level qualifications in their mid-forties or fifties--and they were all men might I add!)

But Coach Krystal, your a SHOW JUMPER. I'm DRESSAGE.

Totally different. Totally.

Oh really? Firstly, show jumping is DRESSAGE with jumps sprinkled in between. If you can't collect your horse, get impulsion, straightness, balance, confidence and correct position, you can't jump.

Period.

Secondly, in order to get my FEI II as a show jumping coach, it was REQUIRED for me to be able to teach to a fairly high level of dressage. In fact, the same level dressage as those who are qualified FEI II Dressage coaches.

But here's the kicker. THEY (the FEI II Dressage Coaches) did NOT have to be able to coach show jumping.

Let me repeat that. I HAD TO BE ABLE TO COACH TO THE SAME LEVEL AND STANDARD AS AN FEI II DRESSAGE COACH BUT THEY DIDN'T HAVE TO BE ABLE TO TEACH THEIR STUDENTS TO JUMP.

That means not only can I teach EXACTLY what those dressage coaches teach to the same level, I also have to be able to teach JUMPERS TOO. Not just to pop over some 2ft stick on the ground. No. For my level II FEI Coaching the students we were coaching during testing needed to be able to jump 1.30m MINIMUM.

That's not something anyone can just roll out of bed with zero training and do. It requires a great deal of skill and technical riding.

So why is it that dressage coaches only have to be able to teach HALF of what I can teach, and yet they get the same level of qualifications as us jumpers? (And we jumpers somehow get less respect from the dressage riders because "we don't do dressage.")

I'm calling B.S.

In my career I have ridden more Grand Prix horses than I can actually name. I have ridden Piaffe. Passage. Heck my 6 year old show jumping mare can do single and double tempi changes (she's still learning so they are far from perfect. But she can DO THEM.)

I've ridden counter canter, canter pirouettes, canter half pass...

I also was offered multiple times to pursue dressage professionally as a career (which I turned down.) I even turned down a job in Greece where I would be training Grand Prix dressage horses every day as my only job. (No mucking stalls or grooming, just riding and training GP horses.)

You might be wondering, how is this possible?

I'll tell you a little secret.

You're not going to like it.

Dressage is just a fancy french word for TRAINING.

THAT is all dressage is. Dressage isn't some special, unique style that only a specific breed of horse or type of rider can do. Nope. Mules can do dressage. 99 year olds can do dressage.

But not everyone can show jump 1.60m. Not every horse can jump that high (or wants to.) Not every rider can either. It takes more than talent to jump a course of 15-20 jumps successfully over fences taller and wider than you are standing upright.

It takes money. Bravery. Skill. Talent and a teeny tiny bit of luck too.

Dressage, in my eyes, is a sport for everyone (though many would have you believe it isn't.) And although nowadays it may seem like only the warmbloods imported from Germany can do dressage, that's actually far from the truth. Any horse and any rider can and SHOULD learn dressage. Does every horse and rider NEED to learn to piaffe and passage? Nope. That's not what dressage is about.

Dressage is also NOT about forcing horses head's down into a "frame" or riding "on the vertical" or riding with spurs and a double bridle. Dressage isn't about judges sitting in a box sharing their opinions.

Dressage at the end of the day boils down to one thing and one thing only.

And that's training.

The good news is, I have an edge and an advantage over any dressage coach you've ever worked with.

You WILL ride over poles. You WILL do things no dressage coach has ever told you to do.

I will CHALLENGE you to question the system (a little bit) and I will open your eyes and mind to think differently and to see dressage as more than just a walk trot intro test with judges beady eyes watching you.

Dressage is about being a team mate with your horse. It's about connection, feeling "one" and together. It's about timing, accuracy, and the ability to do what's best for your horse. It's about being the best for your horse so your horse can shine and be their absolute best for you.

And it's about applying your dressage training to go on and achieve more success in whatever sport you choose than had you only focused on dressage solely and never branched outside your comfort zone, incorporated new training exercises that challenged you and added a splash of FUN in your daily riding routine.

I aim to achieve all that and more with this easy to follow workbook.

If you will trust the process and "Wax on, Wax off" just like the Karate Kid, you WILL see results.

Even though I'm a "show jumper" *GASP!* I hope you keep an open mind and let the results from this book speak for themselves.

To your success!

*Coach Krystal Kelly*

Coach Krystal and "Zefira" at her private show jumping yard in beautiful Spain.

# YOUR BIG WHY

## How to set goals that stick and actually achieve them!

# INTRODUCTION

I'm on the phone a lot with equestrians from all around the world. Working virtually as a coach has really opened up new possibilities that simply didn't exist when I was growing up. I used to have to book flights if I wanted to train with the world's best. Now my clients get to train with the best without leaving their home!

This new world of technology means that I get to talk to riders in unique cultures, time zones and on different continents on a regular basis. It's a lot of fun but it's also very revealing.

The biggest thing I've noticed is that no matter what language they speak, how many years they've been riding, what type of horse they have, if they are beginners or already jumping in the 1.30 classes...

Equestrians have one very similar problem... they ALL get stuck at some point or another. They hit what my team refers to in our office as, "The Rider's Plateau."

What is it?

A lot of us have been riding since we were kids. As kids we could stay on anything, feared nothing and were (annoyingly) naturally talented. But then the years go by. Some of us take a long break from riding only to rediscover the joy again later in life after our kids are grown. Others have had to enjoy horses "on the side."

Some of you ride full time and take whatever you can get. But no matter your story, chances are you're still holding on to certain things which are not serving you or your horse. Things like "bad habits," (which I call "holes in your riding foundation") and the only reason you haven't hit your goals yet is that you need to let go of these bad habits once and for all.

If you don't change something soon, eventually you are going to either burnout or hit that rider's plateau (if you haven't already) where you just can't progress past a certain point or feel like you've reached a ceiling. Or all of the above.

The rider's plateau is when you feel like progress is either not moving at all or it's moving VERY slowly. Slower than butter melts in Antartica.

You want speed! You want to get better! You ride regularly! You take lessons regularly, go to clinics, buy all the stuff you're supposed to buy, try all the gadgets and doodads. You've invested in the fancy horse. Heck, you've even trained with a LITERAL OLYMPIAN!

WHY AM I NOT PROGRESSING?! You drop to your knees and shout to the sky, waving your fists in the air out of frustration.

Ok, some of you are laughing. But others reading might be seriously wondering if I have super spy cameras hidden inside this workbook. (I don't.)

Firstly, take a deep breath! You are not alone.

Just because you've ridden with an Olympian doesn't mean they were a good coach. Great riders are often the lousiest instructors (speaking from experience here. If we ever meet in person don't forget to ask me to tell you the story of that time I worked for an Italian Grand Prix Show

Jumper in Sicily who used to "drink to make the jumps look smaller." Now HE was an AWFUL coach... but man were his horses fabulous!)

It's not your fault that you feel stuck right now!

It happens to everyone. It happens to the best. And if it hasn't happened to you yet, it would have. TA DA! Your magic Genie has arrived and all you had to do was open this book!

The reason many of you are unable to progress past your own invisible glass ceiling is for two reasons.

**Reason #1: You have a lifetime of building incorrect muscle memory.** Once you've engrained that muscle memory into your system, it's difficult for your body to "undo" what you have learned. That is why I cringe whenever I hear beginner riders learning how to ride from YouTubers. I CRINGE. Please don't do that. It's not worth the damage you are doing to your body to get a few "helpful pointers" from someone who probably doesn't even have correct muscle memory themselves (and therefore cannot teach the correct methodology to achieve it.)

What we need to do is RE-PROGRAM your body.

POOF! Your wish is my command! Inside this workbook you will find one new exercise each and every week to help your body RE-PROGRAM. You will find this re-programming exercise each week inside your COOL DOWN section of your training plan.

DO NOT SKIP THIS EXERCISE.

It will seem alarmingly, glaringly simple. You will think to yourself, "I don't need that. It's too obvious. It's too easy."

To that I reply: Have you ever heard the expression, "Eat an apple a day, keep the doctor away?"

What if that were true? What if... you ate an apple every day of your life... and because of it... you never got sick... never suffered from cancer... never got food poisoning... never felt a hangover... never broke a nail... never flattened your ex's tire when you found out he was cheating on you because your heart was never really broken...

Ok, ok, ok. But seriously. What if it were true? Eat an apple a day, keep the doctor away.

It sounds pretty simple to do. It's sort of like common sense really.

And yet how many of us actually DO IT? Any takers?

**DON'T OVERLOOK THE IMPORTANCE OF SOMETHING OR THE VALUE OF AN EXERCISE BASED ON IT SEEMING SIMPLE.**

The question you should be asking me is: Does it work?

And to that I reply, yes. Yes, it does.

**Reason #2: You don't know how to set goals correctly**

What?! What do you mean I don't know how to set goals?! I've told everyone since I was 4 years old that I am going to the Olympics!

There you go waving your fist at me again...

I don't doubt that you THINK you know how to set goals.

But experience speaking to literally thousands of equestrians all around the world in different cultures, time zones and continents has proven to me that...

You don't.

It's time to face the cold hard truth, stop waiting for that butter in Antartica to melt and step into the big leagues.

We wear big girl breeches at the big leagues. And they are ultra soft.

**Here is the incorrect way to set goals:**
Say vague things like, "I want to improve" or "I want to get better" or "I want to ride Grand Prix."

Oh, you do? Great! Tell me how much money you plan on spending to purchase your Grand Prix horse? Are you intending to go for a horse with Flemmingh bloodlines because of the ultra-sensitivity the line produces? Or were you planning for more of a flashy, powerful type like Totilas? Which competitions do you have lined up on your calendar next year to help you qualify? Do you have your FEI registration yet? What about your horse?

There's a big difference between "wishing" and "goal setting."

Goal setting is SPECIFIC. Goal setting is having a PLAN.

You might be thinking, "I don't have the money for an Olympic horse." Well, you have two options. You either need to get the money or you need to face facts that you have wishes, not goals.

That is what we are going to do now. We are going to go deep. Atlantic Ocean deep. Searching for Spanish gold deep.

Deep, deep.

Some of you might very strongly dislike me right now. That's ok. The truth can sting sometimes. I am here to be your Coach, not your friend. That means sometimes I have to play "Good Cop Bad Cop" and be the person that tells you those things no one wants to hear but everyone should.

That's my literal job.

I'm here to support you. Give you the tools you need to succeed. I WANT success for you. If Grand Prix and the Olympics is your goal at the end of the exercise I'm about to give you, I'm ALL FOR IT!

SIGN ME UP TO BE YOUR COACH! I'm a hell yes, 100% all in on my clients type of gal. That's why I tend to work with the truly go-getting types who are serious 100% HELL YES type of A-players.

Not everyone is. And that's ok.

And by the way, there is NO SUCH THING as an unworthy goal. A goal is something extremely personal. It's YOUR goal. Don't let anyone pressure you or tell you what your goal should be. I don't put a filter and choose only the clients that I think have a shot (and the funds) to go Grand Prix.

Truthfully, my clients are typically women ranging from 30-60's, who are amateur riders. They own a lovely horse which they ride 3-5 times a week, they have a full time job or a career outside of horses and they don't have the time to be chasing the Olympics. Most of them have never ridden a Grand Prix horse or a Piaffe in their life. Most of them plateau at 2nd or 3rd level dressage and seem to never be able to move further than that (before me that is.)

And that's ok. I've also worked a lot with rider's of every discipline! I've coached endurance riders, an entire polo club, dressage and show jumping riders, western riders, competitive trail rider's and everything in between. I've had clients as young as 4 and as old as 75 applying these training methods.

The point is. I am not the person to judge you or your goals. I'm not the bad guy! I'm the person to help you with your goals. It's not just my actual business mission statement to help you achieve your goals. It's my life's purpose.

But this workbook is about you, not me.

So now the fun part can start. On the next page I'm going to give you some exercises to help you find your IMPOSSIBLE GOAL and to make that goal, possible.

How this works is easy, let your heart and your mind open to the world of possibilities and trust that your goal (your REAL goal, the secret goal you are scared to tell people about) is in safe hands.

# TURNING THE IMPOSSIBLE INTO
# THE POSSIBLE

**10x is Better than 2x**

A lot of us make the mistake of trying to think of a "realistic goal." That is usually a 2x goal. We try to improve by 1% increments. **Example:** I would like to go from riding a 1st level test to a 2nd level test. That is a realistic goal. I can sign up for a 3 day clinic next month and probably get there. I can keep taking lessons once a week and maybe in 6 months I'll be ready.

That is the prime example of why so many of us get stuck and hit that plateau. That's because, when we set our sights on a "realistic goal" or we try to improve by only small increments like 1% better or 10% better, we are subconsciously setting ourselves up for failure.

It's easier to stay the same than it is to get better. It's easier to not go to the gym than it is to go to the gym just as it's easier to scan Youtube for "helpful tips" or sign up for a 3 day clinic than it is to actually DO WHAT IT TAKES to get better. Does that mean you have to ride 32 horses a day, 29 hours a day, 8 days a week to improve?

NO!

This workbook will have you improving even if you ride 3 times a week. Actually, even if you ride once a week, so long as you apply our methods to the T, they will work. It will take 10x's longer if you only ride once a week, true. But they will still work.

What this means is we need to aim for 10x goals, not 2x goals. We need to shake up our nervous system a little bit. We need to feel slightly nervous, anxious yet also excited about our goals.

No one sprang out of bed at 3 am, dropped $2000 in competition fees, transport fees and did multiple 3 am coffee runs all in the name of "a few helpful tips." Helpful tips (2x goals) that get you "realistic" improvement does not cause your body to tingle. It doesn't cause you to do irrational things like book one way flights, drive across the country, or empty your savings account in order to achieve.

If the goal doesn't scare you just a little bit, it's not big enough. If the goal isn't something you'd spend your life savings to achieve, it's not big enough. If the goal isn't something you'd be willing to make yourself a little uncomfortable for (like waking up at 3am or going to the gym every day) then it's not big enough.

I once had a very lovely client of mine who qualified in the United Kingdom to travel to the USA to compete at the World Equestrian Games. The only problem was, she couldn't afford to fly her horse to the USA and back for a single competition and the UK Equestrian Federation wasn't going to pay for it either.

So you know what she did?

She refinanced her home, booked her horse and her a flight and went to the World Equestrian Games.

It might seem extreme for some, but for her it was the right decision.

Because her goal and dream was stronger than her problem, she found a solution and **she made it happen.**

Another very lovely (and extremely good looking) client of mine decided it was time to buy her dream home (which meant dream equestrian property really). She spent a year searching for the right property until finally, she found it! It was almost as if the property had been built just for her to find it.

There was just one problem.

The property was sold.

Did she pout and go look at other properties? No. That property was her goal.

It just wasn't ready for her yet.

So she made a plan to be ready for the property and guess what, the sale fell through, she bought the property and lived happily ever after.

Her goal was achieved because her goal was very clear, specific and she maintained her laser focus even when the odds seemed against her. She didn't have a "fall back goal." She kept her eye on her goal.

I know, because that woman is me! It was exactly three years ago the first time my husband and I came to visit our beautiful equestrian paradise in sunny Spain. It took us almost a year and a half to purchase the place and another year of struggles once buying the property, but we remained focused because we both knew one thing was certain. This property was our goal. We had been waiting to achieve our goal our entire lives and we weren't going to let a few road bumps and hiccups stand in our way. (If you watched our episode air on International House Hunters on HGTV

Season 188 Episode 12, titled, Horses Before Humans, then you know exactly the kind of struggles I'm speaking about!)

Now it's your turn.

**Use the blank space on the next page to brain dump your IMPOSSIBLE GOALS. The goals that scare you a little. Horse related goals. Financial goals. Career goals. There are no rules. Write down as many as you can think of and BE SPECIFIC. Make them 10x goals.**

# YOUR IMPOSSIBLE GOALS

# IMPOSSIBLE UNLESS...

Now that we've established your IMPOSSIBLE, it's time to discover how to make it POSSIBLE. We are going to take your impossible goals and add the word UNLESS to each of them.

Examples:

My goal of riding at the Monaco Longines is impossible UNLESS I sign up for every Longines Qualifier at Oliva this winter and collect enough points to qualify for Monaco.

My goal of flying my horse to compete in the WEG this year is impossible unless I sell my two new cars and trade them in for junkers and drive those around for the next 2 years until I can save up again for another new car.

My goal of feeling confident and fit enough to jump in the 1.20 classes by the time I'm 55 is impossible unless I hire a nutritionist to help me with my diet, a personal trainer to help me with my fitness, and Coach Krystal to help me with my riding and confidence.

Isn't this a fun game?

Your turn!

# IMPOSSIBLE UNLESS...

Take all your impossible goals and come up with impossible unless ideas. There are no wrong answers! You are simply trying to get those brain juices pumping so you can start to see how possible your impossible goals truly are.

# YOUR NORTH STAR

For the purpose of this workbook, your goal has already been assigned to you. It's the title of this workbook. That is your goal right now and that is your main focus for the duration of the next 4 weeks.

Your North Star, however, is still very important. That is your BIG WHY. The real reason you are really here. It might look like your goal is to master your square halts or be able to have better balance or improve your flying changes. But those reasons are not reason enough. Your North Star is your impossible unless goal you wrote down on the previous page (the biggest horse one you wrote down.)

That North Star is going to be the thing that keeps you focused during this quest. It will keep you on track and it will be the thing that helps you to avoid burn out, fatigue, the rider's plateau and quit-itis.

Keep this goal close to your heart.

Remind yourself of your big goal on every page in your training journal.

You have a mission. A purpose. A life's pursuit.

It's a powerful thing to have a goal and a life's pursuit to work towards.

Cherish it! Embrace it!

And if ever you jump on that Free 1:1 strategy call with me (my gift to you for purchasing this workbook) I hope you share your big secret north star goal with me so we can make a plan as to exactly how we will get you to your destination.

# CONTRACT TO YOURSELF

You must promise to yourself that you will NOT QUIT until you achieve your goal. Remember, you will not fail if you do not quit. So long as you never quit, you will achieve your goal no matter how big or small they may be.

Sign and date below this contract to yourself that you will keep your promise and never quit chasing your North Star.

**My North Star Big Goal Is:**

_____

I, _____, promise to never quit and to make the impossible possible. I will pursue my dream and big goal and enjoy the journey just as much as the destination.

I hereby declare to the universe my word to be true. I am committed to my goal and will do whatever it takes because my dreams are worth it.

**Signature Here:**                              **Date Here:**


_____          _____

# YOUR NEXT 1 YEAR

Now that we know our end goal, you might be wondering... how do I get there? I'm glad you asked! Because that is what my company specializes in.

## Option #1: The Easy, Quicker Way

You can take the easier option and simply hire me and my company to help you achieve your riding goals. We have the training plans, the curriculum and the personalization that is necessary when fast tracking your success. We build your training plans for you and take the burden on our shoulders of actually coming up with the specific steps to getting you there based on your specific needs, your challenges, your goals etc.

## Option #2: The Slower, Harder Way

You can try to do it yourself without any support or guidance. This way takes longer because if you knew how to achieve your goal you would have done it already. There is going to be a long road ahead of trial, error, wrong turns, speed bumps and dead ends. But that's ok! It's YOUR journey and if you are willing to take the dirt road to your goal it's certainly possible if you have the determination and grit necessary to fight your way there.

Now that you know your two options, let's discuss your next 1 year and how you can determine your short term goal to get you 1 step closer to your BIG GOAL.

We achieve this through reverse engineering our BIG GOAL. First, I want you to put a realistic timeline on your big goal (keeping in mind that option 1 gets you there quicker and option 2 much slower if at all.)

**My Timeline for Achieving My Big Goal:** (Example: 10 years, 20 years, 5 years...) Fill in the blank below.

_____

**Next we need to reverse engineer all the things we need to be able to accomplish in order to achieve that goal (just a rough outline, you don't need specifics.)** Example: If you feel 10 years is realistic to achieve your goal, what do you need to be doing 5 years from now? What do you need to be doing this year in order to reach that 5 year milestone? So for example, in 5 years I will be riding FEI classes in Europe. In 2 years I need to already have my own horse which I'm regularly competing in at elementary level so I can build my confidence and experience at that level for at least one year before moving up to the big leagues. In the next 1 year I need to be confidently doing... X.

Now it's your turn! Write your reverse engineering plan below.

_____

_____

_____

_____

_____

_____

_____

**Now that you know your rough plan, write down your goal for the next 1 year below:**

---

Hold onto this goal for the duration of this workbook! This goal is the goal you are working on right now in order to help keep yourself on track to reaching your BIG GOAL.

We can then break down our next 1 year goal into even smaller goals. If you are interested in hiring us, great! Jump on that 1:1 strategy call with us as soon as possible or enroll in our "Sticky Butt Bootcamp" (our non-negotiable rider foundation coaching program.) You can find the QR code at the back of the book or jump here:
**www.theinternationalequestrian.com/freestrategycall**

If you intend on doing it yourself and sticking with option #2 then the good news is we can still help you on your journey. Simply mix and match our various workbooks (you can find them on Amazon and our website www.coachkrystalkellybooks.com).

So for example: if your goal is to ride a Novice Test this year and score 70% or higher, you can build your next 12 months training plan based on your goal using our workbook and coaching system.

For example:
**Month 1-Month 2:** Sticky Butt Bootcamp Coaching **Month 3:** Perfecting Rhythm **Month 4:** Success Mindset **Month 5:** Building Topline **Month 6:** Rider Confidence **Month 7:** Circles and Corners **Month 8:** Mastering Contact **Month 9:** Mastering Impulsion **Month 10:** Mastering Straightness

# EXAMPLE CALENDAR

It's important to create your plan in advance because at some point, you are going to want to give up and quit. You will say to yourself things like, "I'm too busy this week" or "I'm too tired" or "the weathers too bad." YES there is some room for flexibility. This is YOUR calendar and plan after all.

No one from our team is going to call you late at night because you rode on Wednesday when you originally thought to ride on Tuesday. Life happens. We want to avoid the P word.

Procrastination.

We also don't want you to quit! That is why we've put together a handy-dandy calendar for you on the next page. Fill it out with your own plan for the next 28 days. It doesn't need to be detailed (we have the details in this workbook). All you have to do is decide when you are riding and then do your best to hold yourself accountable and make sure you ride the same main session 3x's a week before moving onto the next!

|    | SUN | MON | TUE | WED | THU | FRI | SAT |
|----|-----|-----|-----|-----|-----|-----|-----|
| W1 | Trail Ride | | Mindset Exercise | 1st riding Session | | 2nd riding Session | 3rd riding Session |
| W2 | Mindset Exercise | Trail Ride | | 1st riding Session | | 2nd riding Session | 3rd riding Session |
| W3 | 1st riding Session | | 2nd riding Session | | 3rd riding Session | Family Event | Family Event |
| W4 | Trail Ride | 1st riding Session | | 2nd riding Session | | 3rd riding Session | |

# MY 28 DAY TRAINING CALENDAR

Use the calendar below to outline your next 28 days following our training plan. You should remember to include 3 riding sessions each week (if you ride more feel free to make them free days on the trail or having fun or not working on the program.) If you ride less than 3x's a week then plan it out!

**Month:** _____

**Year:** _____

|      | SUN | MON | TUE | WED | THU | FRI | SAT |
|------|-----|-----|-----|-----|-----|-----|-----|
| W1   |     |     |     |     |     |     |     |
| W2   |     |     |     |     |     |     |     |
| W3   |     |     |     |     |     |     |     |
| W4   |     |     |     |     |     |     |     |
|      |     |     |     |     |     |     |     |

# MY 1 YEAR TRAINING CALENDAR

Use the calendar below to outline your next 1 year following our training plan. Write down each month what workbook you'd like to do for those months (1 of our workbooks = 28 days) or if you plan on joining our Sticky Butt Bootcamp or our 3, 6 or 12 month virtual coaching program, write that down!

**My 1 year goal:**                                    **Year:**

_____              _____

| JAN | FEB | MARCH | APRIL | MAY | JUNE | JULY |
|-----|-----|-------|-------|-----|------|------|
|     |     |       |       |     |      |      |

| AUGUST | SEPT | OCT | NOV | DEC | JAN | FEB |
|--------|------|-----|-----|-----|-----|-----|
|        |      |     |     |     |     |     |

**Notes:**

_____

_____

_____

_____

# HOW TO TAKE FULL ADVANTAGE OF THIS LIFE CHANGING WORKBOOK

# How to Use this Workbook

Just like you, I am OBSESSED with collecting books about how to improve my skills as a rider. I love learning new exercises, collecting helpful tips and adding fresh perspectives to my toolbox. It's helped me a lot over the years.

As much as I love books, they also have one BIG downside to them... there's no realtime support! You do your best to memorize everything word for word so you can later race to the barn and try to apply all the good tips you've learned. But by the time you've saddled up and warmed up, you've forgotten half of it, the other half you "know" in your brain but can't seem to make your body actually DO the thing you just learned.

It can be downright frustrating.

That is why this book is unlike ANY OTHER BOOK that exists. This is NOT a book that you read and memorize and try to apply on your own. We've revolutionized the way equestrians can train at home on their own.

We've done several super awesome, techie and downright cool things that you will discover as you use this workbook (as well as the other workbooks found in our series of workbooks )

**Awesome Bonus #1:**
This is a step by step training plan that has been specifically designed to GET YOU RESULTS. That means that during the next 30 days (or however long you take to complete your workbook) you do not need to spend the time and energy trying to think of your own training plan. Simply do what we say and you will see results.

Have you ever seen the movie, The Karate Kid? Remember Mr. Miyagi, "Wax on, Wax off?" It drove Daniel-son crazy until he realized he had been learning karate the whole time (even when he was waxing cars and painting fences!)

This workbook is like that.

I am the first and ONLY FEI Level II Show Jumping Coach from North America, the UK, & Australia... I've trained 1,000's of horses and students in over 20+ countries around the world in person and 10's of thousands in over 146 countries virtually.

I've been there. I've done it. I've seen it all.

No one on this planet has gone the lengths I will go, spend the amount of money I've spent in order to master the skills I have developed over the last 19+ years I've worked professionally in this industry. I've spent more money and time learning and mastering the art and skills of show jumping than it takes doctors to become a brain surgeon. (Seriously. You can become a brain surgeon in just 14 years and $300,000 tuition fees!)

I've traveled to places most people would be terrified to travel to as a solo female in my 20's in order to train with the best, work for the best and become the best. If there was a guru or different style to learn, I booked a one way flight, no matter the destination, in order to learn this skillset. I've traveled and worked with top show jumpers in countries like Iraq, India, Egypt, Romania, Italy, Belgium, Mongolia, Indonesia and England to name a few.

I'm not telling you this to brag. I'm telling you this because I am going to tell you to "Wax on, Wax off." And just like Daniel-son, some of you will question me. Others will think, "Pshh that exercise is way too easy!" Or "I've done that before" or "I already know that one" or "what does this have to do with a Novice Dressage Test?" or... the list is endless.

The exercises inside this book are not meant to be crazy Christmas-Tree shaped pole exercises requiring 52 poles and 47 cones because it looks AWESOME on Instagram.

F. THAT.

These exercises are not meant to be complicated, "unique," or "new." Why re-invent the wheel I say. Because here's the thing I learned working in over 20+ countries with Grand Prix horses around the globe.

Grand Prix trainers and Olympic riders do NOT have time to set up 52 poles and 47 cones for Instagram. They do NOT re-invent the wheel with "cutesy" exercises they saw on YouTube. They stick to what **works.**

Horses are simple. They have simple needs. It is often us the riders that tend to over-complicate things. We try way too hard because we want so badly to be "good" that we forget that often times the answers are resolved by mastering the basics. That is why during this workbook we will be focusing on:

<u>**QUALITY**</u>
**Over**
**Quantity.**

An Olympic rider can take a single pole on the ground and do 20 different things with it. It doesn't matter if it's a green horse or their top Olympic horse. They STILL use a single pole on the ground to train.

Which brings me to...

**Awesome Bonus #2:**
Self assessments, progress trackers, journal entries and other helpful resources in this workbook to help you improve the QUALITY of your exercises and rides. These are the real treasures inside this workbook. It's not the exercises that will change your life. Anyone can ride over a pole on the ground and check it off their list of "to-do's." But not everyone can ride over that same pole on the ground purposefully, with clear intention and a proven structure that helps them reach new levels and milestones with their horses.

That is why it's important for you to document! Document, document, document! Write down your results. Track your progress. You cannot fail as long as you don't quit. It doesn't matter if the first time you do the exercise you rated yourself a -6 on a scale of 1-5. When you write down your experiences, challenges and goals regularly you will start to notice a pattern. An upward trend of you moving in the right direction.

You will feel more motivated and be more likely to stick with your goal and not get distracted by shiny objects. You will achieve success so long as you follow the system we've laid out for you and you commit to documenting your results and progress no matter how abismal it may feel at times.

**Awesome Bonus #3:**
You are not alone on this journey! As a special bonus we have a community of like-minded equestrians for you to rally moral support and share your wins with. Upload your pics and videos and get replies and motivation from our team of dedicated coaches. (Maybe even me personally if you're lucky!)

Join our FREE facebook group here:
**https://www.facebook.com/groups/theinternationalequestrian**

**Awesome Bonus #4:**
This workbook was designed to take most equestrians 30 days to complete. (Assuming you ride 3 or more times a week. Or 60 days if you only ride once or twice a week.)

We have created this series of Dressage Guide books to support you not just for the next 30 days, but for YEARS to come. We have published over 10 different workbooks in the series. You can mix and match them or choose your favorites and do the same challenges a couple times each year.

That's the beauty of these workbooks! You can build your training plans for the next 1 year, 2 years or 5 years! You can do these exercises multiple times and actually have a record on your shelf documenting the progress you've made over the months and years. That way you never get stuck or hit the dreaded "rider's plateau" and continually have something to work on and improve in a structured and organized way.

If you enjoy these workbooks, **please remember to leave us a positive review on Amazon or our website for a special discount!** This helps other equestrians find our books and helps them on their own journey towards success.

**Awesome Bonus #5: (Optional)**
Even though these workbooks are extremely powerful and will help you immensely, there are some of you who still understand the importance and require the assistance of extra support which is more personalized and tailored to you and your horse's specific needs.

That is where our unique virtual coaching services come in. At The International Equestrian there is an opportunity for those who are truly committed and dedicated to their growth and abundant mindset and skillset development as a rider. We offer a fully built coaching service famously known as our "Sticky Butt Bootcamp" to help you improve your riding and undo years of bad habits and incorrect muscle memory which includes regular 1:1 feedback on your riding videos.

If you are interested or even just curious about how our virtual coaching programs and our Sticky Butt Bootcamp could work for you, I invite you to visit our website using the link below:

**https://www.theinternationalequestrian.com/sticky-butt-bootcamp**

## SCAN ME

**Awesome Bonus #6:**

Audio Lessons are becoming increasingly popular as of late. The funny thing is when we first came up with the idea in 2020 when we started The International Equestrian, everyone had more doubts than ever. It was the pandemic but even on lockdown equestrians had the same question.

How can audio lessons work when my instructor can't see me?!

Now we know better. Audio lessons are not much different than traditional riding lessons. Traditional riding lessons is having your instructor standing in the middle of the arena saying the same things on repeat (or so it seems at times) like "look up!" "stop looking down at your horse" or "sit up" or whatever your nuanced bad habit is that seemingly won't go away no matter how many times your instructor tells you to fix it.

The great advantage to audio lessons is that you can be 100% focused on you and your horse. You don't have to rely on others and you can start to FEEL what's happening underneath you as you follow along to the guided instructions step by step.

Our students have achieved incredible results by following the training plans found inside these workbooks and even greater results when they added our unique Guided Audio Riding Lessons to their riding routines as an extra means of support.

This saves you the hassle and stress of wondering in real-time if you are doing it "right." This saves you the struggle of trying to overcome whatever challenge your horse decides to throw you that day. With our Horse Riding Lessons App you can simply press play on your phone, slip your phone in your breeches pocket and follow along to the calming voice while you work on improving yourself and your horse without any distractions or negative thoughts creeping in.

On the next page you will find our special bonus as to how you can access these audio lessons as well as keep to our recommended audio lesson training plan throughout this journey.

Although this is an optional bonus, it is a huge hit with all our members and clients! The results speak for themselves and it's worth trying it out.

# ◁))) GUIDED AUDIO LESSONS KEY

Throughout this book you will find some helpful badges which name the exact audio lesson (found inside our Horse Riding Lessons App in the App Store for a monthly subscription or available to purchase one-time as a bundle) you can listen to as a means to implement REAL-TIME instruction into your daily rides.

**For those unfamiliar with our Audio Lessons:** The audio lessons are **not** required in order to use this book HOWEVER, we've noticed that those who pair this workbook with our audio lessons see DRASTIC results with their horses! That's because it's easy to forget what's in your book when riding. With the audio lessons you get step-by-step instructions and explainations given to you while you ride your horse.

**For those of you** already using the audio lessons, use this handy key below as a reference to help you stick to your workbook training plan throughout the next 30-60 days. You will find these badges throughout this workbook as a helpful tool with bonus exercises for you to ride along to as well as theory classes and more on the days you don't ride.

## GET OUR AUDIO LESSONS:

**Step 1:** Choose Your Bundle or Purchase them all (Over 200+ audios)
**Step 2:** Get an email with instructions or the audio files
**Step 3:** Choose Your Lesson, Press PLAY & ride to the instructions on your horse

www.coachkrystalkellybooks.com

SCAN ME

Cindi
7h · 🌐

Henry and I did our very first coaching session today. The 6 week challenge: Week 1 - Perfect Warm Up #1
I was absolutely shocked at how much better our upward transitions were after a few minutes. Henry is still learning everything new as he was previously a decent racehorse. He struggles to understand upward into trot and tends on the lazier side. This coaching session was absolutely brilliant down to the "take a deep breath" as at that point he was getting a little flustered and so was I. Thank you Krystal Kelly for this amazing platform. I cannot wait to do my next session on Thursday!

## SCAN ME

5.0 RATING

# Claim your
# $100 Discount

HIGH QUALITY

As a special welcome gift and to thank you for getting my book... I'd like to extend you a very special invitation to get my SUPER effective "Perfect Warmups" guided audio riding lessons bundle for this insanely low price, just go to our website and use code: **forever100** at checkout to save $100...

When you combine my book with this plug-and-play guided audio riding lessons...you literally have a turnkey solution to work every horse you ride CORRECTLY without having to hire expensive "trainers" to sit on your horse for you. You'll master the skillset to help your horse shine their brightest no matter your sport or level!

**www.coachkrystalkellybooks.com**

# Guided Audios Key:

## RIDING LEVEL (Difficulty):

**Level 1**
(Walk & Trot Only)
Ideal for green horses or beginner riders

**Level 2**
Walk, trot & canter

**Level 3**
Introducing more complex exercises

**Level 4**
Advanced
Technical & challenging for both horse & rider

## Lesson Module: (The Section in the App to Find the Lesson)

Rider Balance

Warm Ups / Cool downs

Ride Along Stories

Mounted Games

Dressage

Polework

Classroom Theory

Endurance / Trail

Horse Fitness

## Lesson Duration:

15 minutes       30 minutes       40 minutes       1 hour

 **LOOK OUT FOR THESE HELPFUL TIPS & REMINDERS TO HELP YOU ON YOUR QUEST!**

# RULES:

Every week for the next 28 days, you will be given ONE main exercise. Along with this main exercise you will also be given your warm up and cool down exercises.

**What we expect from you:** You MUST ride the main exercise THREE TIMES before being able to move on to the next exercise! If it takes you 3 weeks, it takes you 3 weeks, but you are not allowed to continue to week 2 until your week 1 tasks are complete. (Some exercises will offer you different variations of the same thing to keep it spicy.)

Wax on, wax off, remember?

Each exercise will have a special training journal for you to fill out after your ride. You will see them labeled as: "Baseline Ride #1," "Establishing Quality Ride #2" & "New Muscle Memory Ride #3." These training journals will exist for each new week during the next 30 days. (If you need extra blank training journal pages you can order our 90 Day Training Journal on Amazon or our website:
### www.coachkrystalkellybooks.com

**The importance of these 3 journal entries and why they are labeled as such:**
**Baseline Ride #1:** The first time you try your exercise for the week, we don't expect it to be perfect. Even if you've done the exercise (or a similar variation in the past) chances are you didn't document it and rate yourself. We need the first ride to be our "establishing our baseline ride." That means we need to "see" where we are at in our riding and training scale. It doesn't matter if you've been riding for 1 year or 10 years. We are not tracking your time spent in the saddle, we are tracking your

skillset and quality of skills in the saddle. That is why this first ride's main focus is for you to simply do the exercise as best you can and then immediately write your results down in your training journal, along with writing down and documenting your rider self-assessment scores.

These numbers are VERY IMPORTANT as they are your baseline. (Or your starting point.) In order to be able to track our progress, we need to establish where we are starting from. Some of you will ace the first exercise and score very high. GREAT! That is your baseline. The question is, how can we improve it? Chances are, it wasn't perfect. So how do we improve YOUR numbers (or your baseline)? Even if it's just got room to improve by 1 point, that 1 point is STILL room for improvement.

Or maybe you scored yourself "Olympic quality" 10 out of 10 on your trusty 20 year old, been-there-done-that-steed. But what about your green 5 year old horse sitting in the pasture looking very cheeky? What score did you get on him?

We are ALL working on something and we ALL have room for improvement so this first ride and training journal page is to simply establish your baseline and numbers so we can work on improving those numbers as we go.

**Establishing Quality Ride #2:** Now that we know our baseline numbers and our starting point, it's time to improve! The second session repeating the same exercise (or maybe even a slightly more challenging variation of the exercise which we will give you options for inside this workbook) is all about IMPROVEMENT. Even micro-improvement is still improvement! We want this second session to be our time to reflect and percolate on what we need to focus on to make it 10x's better & then saddle up and do it! This session is about quality, not quantity and you are expected to keep this session short, sweet, light and fun while at the same time staying focused on structured in your ride to achieve massive results in a fraction of the time.

**New Muscle Memory Ride #3:** This is where we put what you've been practicing to the test and ingrain it into our muscle memory system! This session is simulating that "show day" environment by challenging you and your horse to practice what you've learned in a high adrenaline environment designed to allow you and your horse the chance to shine! This is your first taste at your new "glow up!"

# Example:

**Step 1:** Ride your horse following your Week 1 warm up, main session and cool down assigned exercise for the week.

**Step 2:** Fill out your training journal.

**Step 3:** Fill out your progress tracker.

DATE: _____ HORSE: _____

MY BIG GOAL
_____
_____

TODAY I AM GRATEFUL FOR

01 _____

02 _____

03 _____

TODAY'S EXERCISE & GOALS

01 _____

02 _____

03 _____

ENERGY LEVEL OF HORSE (CIRCLE ONE)

MY HORSE'S MOOD

MY MOOD

WEATHER

NOTES
_____
_____
_____
_____
_____
_____
_____

**WEEK 1 BASELINE RIDE #1**

## WEEK 1
*Progress Tracker*
### SCORE

**What would you rate your QUALITY of performance over this exercise as a rider?** Rate Yourself!
(1 being abysmal, 10 being Bring on the Olympics!

| 1 | 2 | 3 | 4 | 5 | 6 | 7 | 8 | 9 | 10 |

**How was your rhythm, pace & adjustability or overall control of your horse during this exercise?** Rate Yourself!

| 1 | 2 | 3 | 4 | 5 | 6 | 7 | 8 | 9 | 10 |

**How was your accuracy & timing?** (Example: Did you see your distances consistently.) Rate Yourself!

| 1 | 2 | 3 | 4 | 5 | 6 | 7 | 8 | 9 | 10 |

**How was your horse overall?** Rate Yourself!

| 1 | 2 | 3 | 4 | 5 | 6 | 7 | 8 | 9 | 10 |

**How was your ride overall?** Rate Yourself!

| 1 | 2 | 3 | 4 | 5 | 6 | 7 | 8 | 9 | 10 |

**Step 4:** Repeat the same process with the same exercise (with different variations if included) 2 more times before moving on to week 2.

**Bonus Exercises:** You will also find two bonus non-riding homework assignments and exercises inside this workbook. Do them anytime.

# CIRCLES &
# CORNERS

**What is it, why you need to master them and how to achieve mastery.**

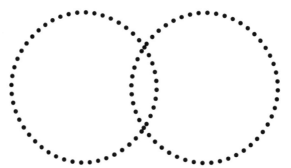

# Circles and Corners

In dressage, circles and corners are key fundamental elements that riders must master to enhance their overall performance and harmony with their horse. For a dressage test, but also for real life scenarios. Without being able to accurately ride a circle or corner, an endurance rider might struggle to serpentine and turn around tight corners, trees and hedges on a fast ride, costing them valuable time and could even cause their horse to fail the vet check. A show jumper will lose precious seconds in a jump off if they are unable to use their aids effectively in order to make the tight turns and corners necessary to win the class.

## Different Sizes of Circles:

In a dressage arena you will typically ride 20m, 15m, or 10m circles however, even if you don't have access to a dressage square it is still important to know what the different size circles FEEL LIKE. Use cones, poles or any other type of marker to map out the different circle sizes in your arena so you can get a feel for the different levels of difficulty.

## Why corners are so difficult:

Corners refer to the 90-degree turns at the ends of the arena, requiring the horse to bend around the rider's inside leg and maintain balance and impulsion throughout the turn. Properly ridden corners should resemble quarter circles, helping to prepare the horse for more complex movements and transitions. Corners are difficult to ride because of the tight angle and many horses will naturally drift, fall to the inside or try to cut the corner. Riding correct corners is an essential part of our training foundation with our horses.

## Why You Need to Master Circles and Corners

- These movements are the foundation and building blocks of training, and the basis for more advanced exercises and movements.

- Proper execution of these basic exercises help to improve the horse's balance and suppleness, enhancing its overall athletic ability and performance.
- It helps maintain a consistent rhythm and tempo. Being able to maintain a consistent rhythm is not only an important part of getting good dressage scores on a test, but it's also vital for jumpers or endurance riders to be able to perform without losing their rhythm or pace. A jumper that loses its rhythm might chip in a stride, lose momentum and have a rail down over a big oxer or even stop and refuse at a fence.
- Practicing these movements sharpens the rider's ability to execute precise and accurate figures, crucial for competition. If you can't ride the basics correctly, you can't ride more technical exercises, period. You can't skip the ABC's and start riding novels without first learning to read and write.
- Working on circles and corners fosters better communication and connection between horse and rider, building trust and responsiveness.
- Mastering the basics prepares the horse for more advanced dressage movements like shoulder-in, travers, and half-pass. Again, you can't skip to "the good stuff" without first mastering those ABC's.

## Common Mistakes
- **Falling In or Out:** This is when the horse leans to the inside or outside, making the circle sloppy and unbalanced. We will be working on getting our communication with our horses and our "walls on" during our warmups so be sure not to skip those inside this workbook!
- **Inconsistent Bend:** Horses and riders are usually right or left handed. You may find throughout this process that you or your horse is better or worse on one side versus the other. We will be working on being more consistent as riders in our warmups and cooldowns inside this workbook.
- **Loss of Rhythm:** We will be working on this a LOT in our warmups and main session. Remember to establish the rhythm you want FIRST and then focus on keeping it and maintaining it versus trying to change it throughout the exercises.

**How this training plan will work for the next 4 weeks and what you can expect to achieve if you stick with it:**

Over the next 4 weeks you will be working on a few things simultaneously.

The first thing will be your warm up sessions. Plan to spend 10-15 minutes each ride on your warm up exercise. The warmup exercises are designed specifically to achieve one clear cut goal: Get you and your horse to be as "one." Riding doesn't mean a thing if your buttons don't work.

Have you ever been on an airplane or maybe seen a movie with pilots prepping for their flight? Before they take off, they have a whole checklist they go through. They push every button, check all the lights and make sure each and every piece of their machine is working as it should.

That is what your warm up exercises are going to be for. Checking all the buttons and making sure you and your horse are fully operational and ready to FLY for your main session.

*Note: Each warm up session can be found inside our Horse Riding Lessons App so you can simply listen to the audio lessons we've assigned for you to assist you in warming up your horse correctly prior to your main exercise.

Next will be your main exercise for the week. This exercise will be a very specific dressage or pole exercise designed to help you achieve your goal.

The main sessions may or may not have the option to continue with a new audio lesson inside our App. If there is no audio lesson for your main exercise, once your warm up is complete the App automatically stops playing and you can continue the main session on your own in peace. If there is a relevant audio lesson, simply go to the lesson we mapped out and press that PLAY button. Follow the instructions as you ride your horse, just like a normal "in-person" lesson.

**It's important not to try to obsess over making the main session "perfect."** Remember, you will repeat each main session 3x's before moving onto your week 2 exercises. You have plenty of time during these 3 rides to improve, practice and perfect it. There is no need to try to overdue it, especially on the first session when introducing the new exercise to you and your horse.

Once your main session is complete (allow yourself anywhere from 15 minutes to 30 minutes to complete this task), you will then move on to your Cool Down assignment.

Give yourself around 5 - 10 minutes to complete your cool down exercise for the week and let your horse stretch and relax after their intense workout. The cool down's main focus is to let your horse stretch, cool down and relax as well as to spend dedicated time each ride to focus on YOU.

It's impossible to help our horses if we need help. Just like on an airplane when the flight attendants tell you to put your own oxygen mask on first before helping a child, we MUST as riders put in the work to improve ourselves just as much as we demand our horse's to work.

It's a two way street! We want our horses to be athletes, we too must be athletes. No exceptions. The cool downs are going to be the perfect chance for you to work on reprogramming your body with correct muscle memory, building and increasing your rider fitness levels and preparing your body for the timing, coordination, strength and balance required to be considered an athlete.

# Circles & Corners
# "Before" Self-Assessment

It's important to see what level you and your horse are at prior to this workbook in order to track your progress. Please rate yourself below. You will do this again at the end of the workbook so you can compare & track your improvement!

**Do you consistently & accurately ride corners and circles?** Rate Yourself! (1 being almost never, 10 being Bring on the Olympics!)

| 1 | 2 | 3 | 4 | 5 | 6 | 7 | 8 | 9 | 10 |
|---|---|---|---|---|---|---|---|---|----|

**How often would you say your horse leans on circles and turns or falls in or out in turns?** Rate Yourself! (1 being frequently, 10 being never.)

| 1 | 2 | 3 | 4 | 5 | 6 | 7 | 8 | 9 | 10 |
|---|---|---|---|---|---|---|---|---|----|

**How is your position and balance?** (Example: Do you fall behind the motion of the horse or struggle in canter?) Rate Yourself!

| 1 | 2 | 3 | 4 | 5 | 6 | 7 | 8 | 9 | 10 |
|---|---|---|---|---|---|---|---|---|----|

**How often do you and your horse "argue?"** Rate Yourself!

| 1 | 2 | 3 | 4 | 5 | 6 | 7 | 8 | 9 | 10 |
|---|---|---|---|---|---|---|---|---|----|

**How would you rate your overall riding ability?** Rate Yourself!

| 1 | 2 | 3 | 4 | 5 | 6 | 7 | 8 | 9 | 10 |
|---|---|---|---|---|---|---|---|---|----|

# TURN IN YOUR #HOMEWORK

Inside our Private Facebook Group you have the opportunity to post your riding videos in order for the chance to get 1:1 feedback from a real FEI Coach! It doesn't matter which of our workbooks you are currently doing, or which week you are on, we accept riding videos from any week so long as you are following our training plans!

**How to Turn in your Riding Videos & Homework:**

https://www.facebook.com/groups/theinternationalequestrian

**Step 1:** Join our facebook group
**Step 2:** Turn in your riding videos & #homework in the group
**Step 3:** If you are lucky, you'll get feedback from a real FEI Coach!

"Hohooo I am controlling my horse s speed! BIG DISCOVERY ( after finishing W5 of sticky butt) when I RIDE ACTIVELY all the way to the fence my spicy mare follows MY RHYTHM and doesnt speed up!!!! I can't believe it how come I didn't figure it out myself??? Thank you Krystal Kelly !!!"
- Kristýna from Czech Republic

# WEEK 1

Your mission for week 1 is to establish your baseline & unlock your hidden potential.

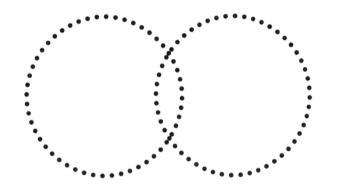

# Motivational Quotes to Pump You Up For Week 1!

"Here's to the crazy ones. The misfits. The rebels. The troublemakers. The round pegs in the square holes. The ones who see things differently. They're not fond of rules. And they have no respect for the status quo. You can quote them, disagree with them, glorify or vilify them. About the only thing you can't do is ignore them. Because they change things. They push the human race forward. And while some may see them as the crazy ones, we see genius. Because the people who are crazy enough to think they can change the world, are the ones who do." – Steve Jobs

"Start where you are. Use what you have. Do what you can." – Arthur Ashe

"Go confidently in the direction of your dreams! Live the life you've imagined!" – Thoreau

"Don't think about your errors or failures; otherwise, you'll never do a thing." – Bill Murray

"Many people think they want things, but they don't really have the strength, the discipline. They are weak. I believe that you get what you want, if you want it badly enough." – Sophia Loren

# Your Road Map to Success

 You are here. →

## FIRST WEEK

- Establishing your baseline
- Relaxing warmup stretches to loosen tightness, stiffness & tension.
- Establishing new routine
- Breaking it all down so we can rebuild you back up

**1**

## SECOND WEEK

- Re-programming muscle memory
- Finding your center & balance
- Establishing partnership with your horse
- Building horse & rider fitness

**2**

**3**

## THIRD WEEK

- Spicing things up and adding a new layer of difficulty
- Establishing quality with more technical exercises
- Pushing you to be the best you can be

## FOURTH WEEK

- Test week
- "Show day" simulation training - putting it all together
- New habits, muscle memory and fitness kicks in
- Technical Riding

**4**

www.theinternationalequestrian.com

# INTRODUCTION TO THE PERFECT WARMUP

"Krystal, what the hell was that?" My hot-tempered, Italian boss shouted at me. It was my first week of work at this gorgeous private show jumping stable, nestled on the hillside overlooking the Mediterranean sea, and already my boss was annoyed with me.

"Umm..." I stumbled for words. I'd only just sat on the horse for 10 minutes when he stopped me. I was 22 years old at the time, and although this was already the fifth country I'd worked at high level show jumping yards, I still had much to learn.

"That's no way to warm up a horse," His hands began waving in that Italian-style that I'd, until now, only witnessed in movies.

I had mounted the horse and only thus far walked him on the buckle one round each direction, and trotted on the buckle with the horse stretching to the floor in each direction. After I'd done the same in canter, I'd assumed my warm-up was done and had begun to pick up the reins.

"You can't just float around the arena on the rail!" He cried. "You must be interesting." My eyebrow pricked, ready to receive further instruction.

"Krystal, bella," his italian charm kicked in. "I want no less than 100 transitions in the next 10 minutes. This horse's hooves must have touched every inch of the arena at least once, and not more than twice." He pointed to the rail, motioning for me to start. "And don't even think about staying on the rail for more than a stride or two!"

Since that day, I never again had another Olympian or top Grand Prix Coach question my warmups.

Later, while working with one of the highest level FEI coaches in the world--the highest being FEI level III of which I'm currently a Level II preparing to get my Level III--a similar story was shared with me, "The warm up is just like a pilot about to fly a plane. The pilot checks all the lights, pushes all the buttons and checks that everything is working before taking off."

The ideal warm-up for a horse has two parts to it. The first part is relaxation and stretching (the one-thing I had done correctly in my Italian boss's eyes that day). This allows the horse's muscles to loosen up, their joints to move and their backs and muscles to literally "warm," just like humans stretch before going for a long run or lifting heavy weights.

The second part of the warm up is not to teach the horse anything new (that is for your working session) but to simply check the engine lights, look for a full tank of gas, be mindful of any warning lights and test that all the installed buttons are working.

A warm-up, when done properly makes for an engaged and interested horse, and also one that is less likely to get injured, or disagree with you later on when you go to teach them something new or perfect what they already know.

That is why, we will be focusing not only on the "meat of the ride" (your main session) but we are going to spend a little time in your warm-up doing a pre-flight check. We want to put a little bit of love into our warm ups and that is why I invented what we like to call, **The Perfect Warm Up**.

Each week you will be assigned a new warm up exercise to implement into your daily routine. These are non-negotiable! There is absolutely no point flipping to the exciting part of the workbook (the part with all the jumps and poles) and going at it on your own.

My guess is, that's what you've already been doing all these years. And how's that been working out for you? Not great?

That's because so many riders focus their attention on the "fun stuff" that they forget that TRUE riding is not won with the jumps, or the test or the fitness, but with the turns, the accuracy, and the precision.

Horse riding is an incredibly technical sport. That's what we love most about it! It's very difficult to "fake" being a top rider. That's because even a 17 million dollar horse can't do all the work for you. If the rider is not setting the horse up for success, eventually the horse's training will regress. Sure, for 17 million, you could probably do better than most, but it still can't do all the work for you. You have to learn how to set your horse up for success if you truly want to win.

The rider's who can achieve this with the most consistency are often the rider's bringing home the $100,000 prize money. THAT is why these warm ups are so important! Now it's time for you to get your exercise for the week and go ride your horse.

Enjoy!

**\*SPECIAL BONUS\*** Remember the Guided Audio Lesson Key at the beginning of the workbook? Every warm up exercise can be found as an audio lesson inside our Horse Riding Lessons App or available for purchase on our website: www.coachkrystalkellybooks.com. Have fun!

# WEEK 1
# WARMUP LESSON PLAN

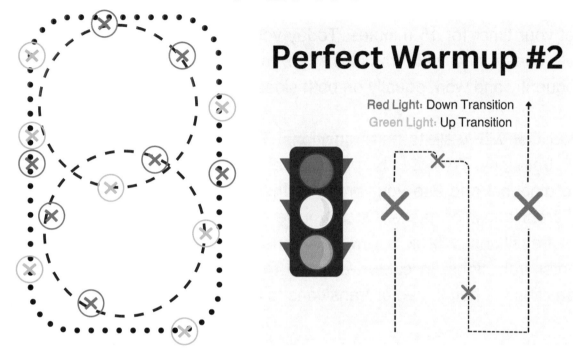

## Perfect Warmup #2

Red Light: Down Transition
Green Light: Up Transition

## The Perfect Warm Up #2

15 minutes

QUICK TIPS

**IMPROVE YOUR ACCURACY BY SETTING SPECIFIC TARGETS. FOR EXAMPLE "I WILL MAKE A TRANSISTION AT EVERY DRESSAGE LETTER. OR MAYBE EVERY OTHER FENCE POST. GET CREATIVE AND TRY NOT TO BE "PREDICTABLE." KEEP YOUR HORSE'S EARS ON YOU THE ENTIRE WARM UP WITHOUT GETTING DISTRACTED AND YOU'LL KNOW YOU HAVE SUCCEEDED!**

**Instructions:**

Spend the first 5 minutes allowing your horse to walk and trot (and possibly canter) on the buckle. Allow them to strech long and low. This will help them to lift their backs and warm them to prepare for the ride ahead.

Set your timer for 15 minutes. Today you will be doing a mixture of walk, trot, canter and halt transitions so make sure you change direction frequently and work equally on both sides!

Start first with walk to halt transitions. To spice things up ask for one or two trot steps. Try not to be predictable! Circle, make figure 8's, go across the diagonal and use your arena to the fullest throughout each of these different transition tasks. Once you've finished in walk move on to walk trot transitions. Mix in a few halt transitions before proceeding to walk canter transitions. In canter feel free to also mix in a few canter to halt transitions or halt to canter transitions to keep things interesting.

Once the timer has gone off you are finished! You can now move onto your main session exercise for the day.

**Benefits of this exercise:**
- Energizes your horse (great for lazy horses!)
- Helps hot horses to stay focused and relaxed (by keeping them busy they feel more at peace. That's because a bored horse is a naughty horse!)
- Establishes your pre-flight check and gets the buttons working
- Keeps things interesting and fun for horse and rider
- Helps horses to put their weight on their haunches to "sit" rather than pull forward or down onto the forehand
- Helps establish soft rein contact (no pulling or heavy horses!)

# WEEK 1
# LONG LINE OF POLES ON A CURVE

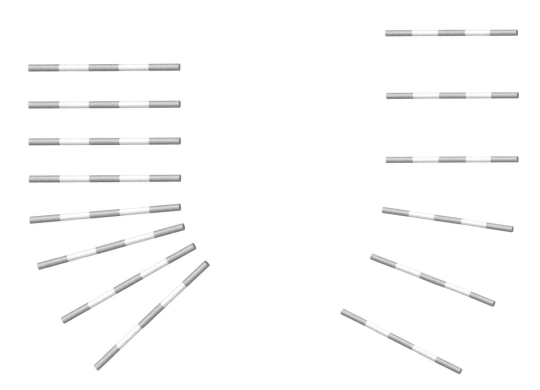

## Equipment Needed:

- AS MANY POLES AS YOU HAVE!
- *OPTIONAL* FOR ALTERNATING RAISED TROT POLES USE BLOCKS

## Set Up:

- TROT POLES: 4 STEPS HEEL TO TOE FROM CENTER OF THE POLE TO CENTER OF THE NEXT POLE (5 STEPS IF YOUR FOOT IS TINY OR YOUR HORSE IS BIG!)
- CANTER POLES 3 METERS BETWEEN POLES (CENTER TO CENTER)

# WEEK 1
# VARIATIONS

## 1st Ride: Long Line of Trot Poles *Optional Walk Poles*

Long line of trot poles to be ridden from both the right and left rein and each direction. You can also choose to first do this exercise in walk only or even in hand with your horse. Walking and in hand work is great for introducing the exercise the first time around.

## 2nd Ride: Alternating Raised

Use blocks to raise each pole on one side so that the center path of the poles is low to the ground. This gives the horse the illusion of an X and helps them pick their feet up and use their back muscles and top line.

## 3rd Ride: Long Line of Canter Poles

Adjust the distance between the poles (or remove some) to create a long line of canter poles. Ride the exercise both directions and from each rein.

You can also divide the arena into a mini-"course" of poles so several canter poles on a curve on one end of the arena, curved trot poles on the other. Mix and match and do the exercise from both directions and alternating between canter and trot.

# WEEK 1
# MAIN EXERCISE

**Helpful Tips:**
- Let your horse figure out the poles! Don't try to interfere or fuss with them. You can keep them straight in the center of the poles and keep them from drifting or from going too fast but otherwise don't try to "help them." Let them sort their own legs out.
- Look with your eyes and heart around the turn, not down at your horse or the poles

**Common Mistakes:**
- Not keeping outside rein and leg contact in the curve
- Looking down at the poles
- Trying to use your inside rein to steer rather than your outside rein
- Not keeping your rein and leg contact throughout the exercise which can cause the horse to drift or speed up / slow down
- Not allowing the horse the chance to "figure it out" and think for themselves! We want our horses to have a brain! Don't try to do all the thinking for them.

**Benefits of this Exercise:**
- Builds top line muscles.
- Helps horses lift their backs and use their abs and core
- Allows the rider the chance to work on their own balance and position

**YOUNG HORSES CAN ACT LIKE THEY DON'T KNOW WHAT TO DO WITH FOUR LEGS! THAT'S ACTUALLY NORMAL. POLE EXERCISES CAN HELP THEM FIGURE OUT WHERE TO PUT THEIR FEET AND HELPS TO CREATE COORDINATION IN THEIR BODY.**

## Instructions:

Pick up trot and establish a good rhythm that is neither fast nor slow.

Ensure you focus on the quality of the trot before approaching the long line of poles, getting an active "springy" trot stride (that isn't too speedy.) You should feel their power coming from the engine in the back. It should feel upwards, maybe even a little "bouncy."

Once you've established the rhythm you want, approach the exercise from both directions. You can place this exercise in the center of the arena, down the long side or in different places of the arena in order to add variety. Mix and match which direction you approach as well as which rein. Keep it interesting! Don't be predictable or boring to your horse.

Keep your horse straight over the exercise, focusing on riding the center of the poles throughout. Plan your turns and be there to support your horse with your rein and leg aids acting as your "walls."

Ride over the exercise for at least 5-10 minutes on each side (taking regular walk breaks as needed.) You should maintain a nice rhythmical stride throughout the entire exercise.

End on a good note and give your horse a big pat and a scratch for a job well done!

Repeat the same exercise over your canter poles. You can choose to spread out the trot and canter poles on different days or combine them and have your trot poles on one side of the arena, canter poles on the other.

# WEEK 1
# COOL DOWN LESSON PLAN

**Neck Stretches**

Week 1 is our gentle stretches week. This week is designed to help your body undo all the years of aches and pains, tension and stress we have built up over the years. Many of us have suffered from previous injuries or bad falls.  For some it's not injury related but simply the stiffness and soreness of getting older or sitting at a desk most of the day.

**Instructions:**
Today's cool down exercise is for YOU, not your horse. Your horse need only walk on the buckle. Allow your horse to stretch their necks down and relax. Keep them walking in a nice swingy walk gait, but don't stress or worry about where they are going. They have the freedom to follow the rail mindlessly while you use this opportunity to focus on your own body, healing and relaxation.

**How to do Neck Stretches:**

Place your reins somewhere where they won't slip down (tuck it over your half pad or hold the reins loosely with one hand, swapping hands as you do the exercise.) You can do this exercise with two different variations. One variation is to simply roll your neck in large circles to the right 10 times and then repeat to the left 10 times.

The second variation is to raise your right arm above your head and gently turn your ear towards your right shoulder, placing your right hand on your head and allowing gravity to stretch your neck to the side. Hold for 10 seconds or a circle then repeat on the other side.

Enjoy the stretch! Let your body dictate your movements. It's not a contest to see how flexible you are. It's the time and space for you to get to know your body and feed it what it needs. If this exercise brings out some discomfort then most likely this exercise is exactly what you need! *Note: You should never feel pain. If there is pain do what is comfortable for your body.*

**Benefits of this exercise:**
- Relieves neck pain
- Deepens seat
- Connects rider with horse
- Strengthens core
- Relaxes your head and neck
- Allows you the chance to breathe deeply and find relaxation in your body and through your horse's body
- Fights stress
- Centers you

# WEEK 1
# BONUS MINDSET /
# NON-RIDING EXERCISE

**Eye Yoga Exercise - V-Shape**

Eye Yoga has been proven to help strengthen eyes and even improve eyesight. As a certified yoga teacher, I'm happy to say I've had a student go down in their eye glass prescription after just 6 months! Eye yoga has never been more important than it is today due to the eye strain we get by staring at screens all day (whether it be playing on our phones, televisions and iPads, or sitting at a desk working on a computer all day.) Even books are no longer books, they are also screens!

Complete the following Eye Yoga Exercise. We recommend once daily for 5 minutes or anytime you start to feel eye strain from screen watching.

**Instructions:**
Sit comfortably and raise your arm in front of you and spread your arms wide until they make a V. Make a thumbs up with your fist. They should be visible out of the corner of your eye. Then you will look at your thumb on the right and then the left. Do this 10 times then swap left to right. The key thing to remember is to not move your head or neck! This exercise should only be done with your eyes.

Want more of these? Find our **10 Minute Easy Eye Yoga book on Amazon by Krystal Kelly.**

# WEEK 1
# MINDSET HOMEWORK

Complete your mindset homework assignment for this week using the blank page below.

DATE: _____ HORSE: _____

## MY BIG GOAL
_____
_____

## TODAY I AM GRATEFUL FOR
01 _____
02 _____
03 _____

## TODAY'S EXERCISE & GOALS
_____
01 _____
02 _____
03 _____

### ENERGY LEVEL OF HORSE (CIRCLE ONE)

## MY HORSE'S MOOD

## MY MOOD

## WEATHER

**WEEK 1 BASELINE RIDE #1**

NOTES
_____
_____
_____
_____
_____
_____
_____
_____
_____

# WEEK 1
## *Progress Tracker*
## SCORE

**What would you rate your QUALITY of performance over this exercise as a rider?** Rate Yourself!
(1 being abysmal, 10 being Bring on the Olympics!

| 1 | 2 | 3 | 4 | 5 | 6 | 7 | 8 | 9 | 10 |
|---|---|---|---|---|---|---|---|---|----|

**How was your rhythm, pace & adjustability or overall control of your horse during this exercise?** Rate Yourself!

| 1 | 2 | 3 | 4 | 5 | 6 | 7 | 8 | 9 | 10 |
|---|---|---|---|---|---|---|---|---|----|

**How was your accuracy & timing?** (Example: Were you able to get the movements on the exact letter.) Rate Yourself!

| 1 | 2 | 3 | 4 | 5 | 6 | 7 | 8 | 9 | 10 |
|---|---|---|---|---|---|---|---|---|----|

**How was your horse overall?** Rate Yourself!

| 1 | 2 | 3 | 4 | 5 | 6 | 7 | 8 | 9 | 10 |
|---|---|---|---|---|---|---|---|---|----|

**How was your ride overall?** Rate Yourself!

| 1 | 2 | 3 | 4 | 5 | 6 | 7 | 8 | 9 | 10 |
|---|---|---|---|---|---|---|---|---|----|

DATE: _____     HORSE: _____

MY BIG GOAL
_____
_____

TODAY I AM GRATEFUL FOR
01 _____
02 _____
03 _____

TODAY'S EXERCISE & GOALS
_____
01 _____
02 _____
03 _____

ENERGY LEVEL OF HORSE (CIRCLE ONE)

MY HORSE'S MOOD                    NOTES
                                   _____
                                   _____
MY MOOD                            _____
                                   _____
                                   _____
WEATHER                            _____
                                   _____
                                   _____
                                   _____
                                   _____
                                   _____

DATE: _____ HORSE: _____

## MY BIG GOAL
_____
_____

## TODAY I AM GRATEFUL FOR
01 _____
02 _____
03 _____

## TODAY'S EXERCISE & GOALS
01 _____
02 _____
03 _____

### ENERGY LEVEL OF HORSE (CIRCLE ONE)

## MY HORSE'S MOOD

## MY MOOD

## WEATHER

## NOTES
_____
_____
_____
_____
_____
_____
_____
_____
_____

www.THEINTERNATIONALEQUESTRIAN.com

# WEEK 1
## *Progress Tracker*
## SCORE

**What would you rate your QUALITY of performance over this exercise as a rider?** Rate Yourself!
(1 being abysmal, 10 being Bring on the Olympics!

| 1 | 2 | 3 | 4 | 5 | 6 | 7 | 8 | 9 | 10 |

**How was your rhythm, pace & adjustability or overall control of your horse during this exercise?** Rate Yourself!

| 1 | 2 | 3 | 4 | 5 | 6 | 7 | 8 | 9 | 10 |

**How was your accuracy & timing?** (Example: Were you able to get the movements on the exact letter.) Rate Yourself!

| 1 | 2 | 3 | 4 | 5 | 6 | 7 | 8 | 9 | 10 |

**How was your horse overall?** Rate Yourself!

| 1 | 2 | 3 | 4 | 5 | 6 | 7 | 8 | 9 | 10 |

**How was your ride overall?** Rate Yourself!

| 1 | 2 | 3 | 4 | 5 | 6 | 7 | 8 | 9 | 10 |

# WEEK 1
# AFTER WEEK REFLECTION
DOCUMENT YOUR PROGRESS!

WHAT HAS BEEN MY BIGGEST STRUGGLE SO FAR?

WHAT IS ONE UNEXPECTED DISCOVERY OR LIGHTBULB MOMENT I HAD THIS WEEK?

WHAT HAS BEEN MY BIGGEST WIN THIS WEEK?

HOW CAN I IMPROVE NEXT WEEK?

WHAT QUESTION COULD I ASK IN THE GROUP OR TO THE INTERNATIONAL EQUESTRIAN TEAM TO HELP ME ON MY QUEST?

# WEEK 2

Your mission for week 2 is to step outside your comfort zone and go after what you want.

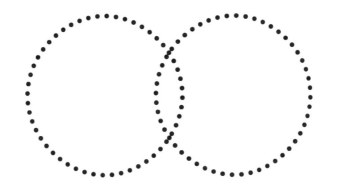

# Motivational Quotes to Pump You Up For Week 2!

"I don't count my sit-ups; I only start counting when it starts hurting because they're the only ones that count." – Muhammad Ali

"I have not failed. I've just found 10,000 ways that won't work." – Thomas Edison

"If you are not willing to risk the usual, you will have to settle for the ordinary." – Jim Rohn

"Fortune sides with him who dares." – Virgil

"Time is more valuable than money. You can get more money, but you cannot get more time." – Jim Rohn

"The more you learn, the more you earn." – Warren Buffett

"What you lack in talent can be made up with desire, hustle and giving 110% all the time." – Don Zimmer

"I've got a dream that's worth more than my sleep." – Unknown

"The struggle you're in today is developing the strength you need for tomorrow. Don't give up." – Robert Tew

# Your Road Map to Success

## You are here.

**1**

### FIRST WEEK

- Establishing your baseline
- Relaxing warmup stretches to loosen tightness, stiffness & tension.
- Establishing new routine
- Breaking it all down so we can rebuild you back up

### SECOND WEEK

- Re-programming muscle memory
- Finding your center & balance
- Establishing partnership with your horse
- Building horse & rider fitness

**2**

**3**

### THIRD WEEK

- Spicing things up and adding a new layer of difficulty
- Establishing quality with more technical exercises
- Pushing you to be the best you can be

### FOURTH WEEK

- Test week
- "Show day" simulation training - putting it all together
- New habits, muscle memory and fitness kicks in
- Technical Riding

**4**

# WEEK 2
# WARMUP LESSON PLAN

## Turn on Haunches

**LISTEN TO OUR INTERACTIVE RIDE ALONG STORY "RIDING TO ALADDIN'S PALACE IN UZBEKISTAN" TO PUT THIS LESSON INTO ACTION!**

**Instructions:**

Spend the first 5 minutes allowing your horse to walk and trot (and possibly canter) on the buckle. Allow them to strech long and low. This will help them to lift their backs and warm them to prepare for the ride ahead. Next, gather your reins until you have a light and soft contact in your hands. If you are not taking advantage of the audio lessons inside our App, set a timer on your phone for 15 minutes.

Today you will be working on being able to pivot the horse's forehand around the hindquarters by making a small circle with the inside foreleg with the horse bending in the direction of the turn.

First establish an active walk. They should feel springy in their steps and light in the front. Make sure you are not next to the rail for this exercise, riding only in the center of the arena. Next, ask for a halt and the turn on haunches. Start this exercise with just doing 90 degree turns. Praise your horse dramatically after you have come back to a halt. You can eventually work up to doing 180 degree turns and then of course a full 360 degrees.

Then mix and match walking and trotting around the arena and halting and doing a turn on the haunches here and there to mix things up.

Once the timer has gone off you are finished! You can now move onto your main session exercise for the day.

**Benefits of this exercise:**
- Establishes your pre-flight check and gets the buttons working
- Helps improve their turns & rollbacks for future
- Help horse to improve canter transitions or problems when picking up the correct lead.
- Help rider with coordination of aids.

# WEEK 2
# S-CHUTE

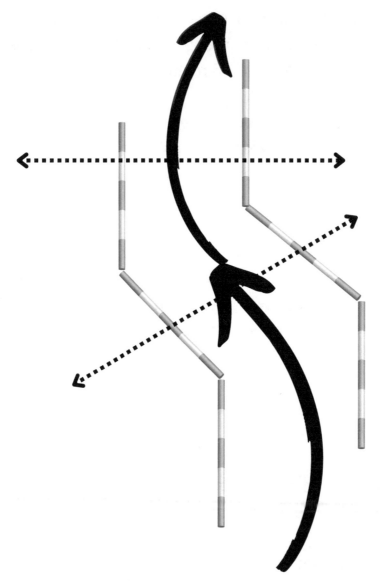

## Equipment Needed:

- 6 POLES

# WEEK 2
# VARIATIONS

## 1st Ride: Walk Trot

Use this time to focus on your position, balance and coordination of aids. Add in transitions and ride over the poles and inside the chute.

## 2nd Ride: Canter

Ride your pole exercise in canter, focusing on maintaining an easy rhythm. Keep the turns smooth and place the poles at least 3 meters apart so you can also canter over the poles.

## 3rd Ride: Leg yields

Inside the chute leg yield your horse into your outside rein and focus on the quality of the bend. If you are more advanced you can do the chute as counter canter or mini-half passes inside the chute. The 3rd session is for you to try to increase the level of difficulty and refine as much as you can. Make sure you do some zig zag leg yields or half passes (only 2-3 steps each side) before entering your chute to be sure the buttons are working first. You can also choose to only do it in walk.

## Other Options:

Move the chute to different places in the arena, add some cones before and after to add halt transitions or rein back. Make the poles wider or more narrow or increase or decrease the angles to add more or less difficulty. You can also make the chute longer by adding more poles to keep the zig zag turns going for longer!

# WEEK 2
# MAIN EXERCISE

**Helpful Tips:**

- Focus on mainting forward motion inside your chute. You don't want your horse to get "sticky" by slowing or speeding up. Focus on your breathing and maintaining that steady rhythm.
- Inside leg, outside rein! Focus on pushing your horse from your inside to your outside without letting them drift outside your outside "walls."

**Common Mistakes:**

- Steering or turning your horse's head and not their body. They need to turn balanced, without leaning or falling to the inside like a motorcycle. Think "turn like a train." This will help keep them upright and balanced.
- Dropping your shoulder in the turns or looking down at your poles or exercise. Keep your eyes looking at a focal point ahead of you.

**Benefits of this Exercise:**

- Helps improve your horse being "between your aids." It gives riders a visual "wall" (of poles) which can later be turned into an invisible "wall" of just your aids (and no poles or rail to depend on!)
- Increases flexibility and suppleness in your horse.
- Adds variety to your ride.

 **YOUR HORSE'S BEND SHOULD BE FROM THE EARS TO THE TAIL, THEIR BODY FEELING WRAPPED AROUND YOUR INSIDE LEG. TRY NOT TO OVER BEND THE HEAD AND NECK AND INSTEAD KEEP THE BEND FROM EARS TO TAIL EQUAL.**

## Instructions:

You will build up this grid incrementally so first start with your normal warm up routine and then ride over your grid as poles on the ground. Then begin building it up to the bounce, then the 1 stride and finally the 2 stride. This exercise will require a helper so be sure to plan having someone on the ground.

This grid exercise was designed for you to approach in trot so you don't have to worry about if you are getting the correct stride into the grid. That means you can focus purely on getting a nice active trot stride and coming into the grid allowing your horse to canter and do all the hard work. Use the time to focus on yourself, especially sitting in the saddle in between the 1 stride and the 2 stride verticals so you can practice your balance.

Always alternate right rein and left rein and remember not to over do the exercise. You want to end on a good note and focus on QUALITY over QUANTITY. You can also adjust the grid to approach in canter and remove your trot poles if you want during your second or third ride. This will affect the distances however so make sure you set it up for a canter approach in this scenario.

This exercise is great for getting the horse to tuck their legs and pick up their feet over the jumps. Use this time to let your horse focus on themselves and their form while you focus on yourself.

Ride over the exercise for at least 5-10 minutes on each side (taking regular walk breaks as needed.)

# WEEK 2
# COOL DOWN LESSON PLAN

**Airplane with a Twist - Sitting Trot**

Week 2 is our gentle stretches week. This week is designed to help your body undo all the years of aches and pains, tension and stress we have built up over the years. Many of us have suffered from previous injuries or bad falls.  For some it's not injury related but simply the stiffness and soreness of getting older or sitting at a desk most of the day.

**Instructions:**
Today's cool down exercise is for YOU, not your horse. Your horse need only walk on the buckle. Allow your horse to stretch their necks down and relax. Keep them walking in a nice swingy walk gait, but don't stress or worry about where they are going. They have the freedom to follow the rail mindlessly while you use this opportunity to focus on your own body, healing and relaxation.

**How to do Airplane with a Twist:**

Place your reins somewhere where they won't slip down (tuck it over your half pad or hold the reins loosely with one hand, swapping hands as you do the exercise.) Stretch both arms out wide to the side and let them pull in opposite directions as if someone is trying to make your arms longer. Then twist your torso until your fingers are facing your horses ears and tail. Twist to the other side. Repeat as many times as needed for at least one lap each direction.

While sitting to the trot try not to obsess over having the "perfect position." Instead use this as an opportunity to explore your body, find those seat bones and let your legs relax and hang comfortable around the belly of your horse.

Enjoy the stretch! Let your body dictate your movements. It's not a contest to see how flexible you are. It's the time and space for you to get to know your body and feed it what it needs. If this exercise brings out some discomfort then most likely this exercise is exactly what you need! *Note: You should never feel pain. If there is pain do what is comfortable for your body.*

**Benefits of this exercise:**
- Opens shoulders
- Relieves lower back pain
- Deepens seat
- Connects rider with horse
- Strengthens core
- Tones & engages lower back and sides
- Burns belly fat
- Fights stress

DATE: _____   HORSE: _____

## MY BIG GOAL

_____

_____

## TODAY I AM GRATEFUL FOR

01 _____

02 _____

03 _____

## TODAY'S EXERCISE & GOALS

01 _____

02 _____

03 _____

### ENERGY LEVEL OF HORSE (CIRCLE ONE)

## MY HORSE'S MOOD

## MY MOOD

## WEATHER

**WEEK 2 BASELINE RIDE #1**

## NOTES

_____

_____

_____

_____

_____

_____

_____

_____

_____

_____

# WEEK 2

# *Progress Tracker*

# SCORE

**What would you rate your QUALITY of performance over this exercise as a rider?** Rate Yourself!

(1 being abysmal, 10 being Bring on the Olympics!

| 1 | 2 | 3 | 4 | 5 | 6 | 7 | 8 | 9 | 10 |
|---|---|---|---|---|---|---|---|---|----|

**How was your rhythm, pace & adjustability or overall control of your horse during this exercise?** Rate Yourself!

| 1 | 2 | 3 | 4 | 5 | 6 | 7 | 8 | 9 | 10 |
|---|---|---|---|---|---|---|---|---|----|

**How was your accuracy & timing?** (Example: Were you able to get the movements on the exact letter.) Rate Yourself!

| 1 | 2 | 3 | 4 | 5 | 6 | 7 | 8 | 9 | 10 |
|---|---|---|---|---|---|---|---|---|----|

**How was your horse overall?** Rate Yourself!

| 1 | 2 | 3 | 4 | 5 | 6 | 7 | 8 | 9 | 10 |
|---|---|---|---|---|---|---|---|---|----|

**How was your ride overall?** Rate Yourself!

| 1 | 2 | 3 | 4 | 5 | 6 | 7 | 8 | 9 | 10 |
|---|---|---|---|---|---|---|---|---|----|

DATE: _____ HORSE: _____

MY BIG GOAL
_____
_____

TODAY I AM GRATEFUL FOR
01 _____
02 _____
03 _____

TODAY'S EXERCISE & GOALS
01 _____
02 _____
03 _____

## ENERGY LEVEL OF HORSE (CIRCLE ONE)

MY HORSE'S MOOD

NOTES
_____
_____

MY MOOD
_____
_____

WEATHER
_____
_____
_____
_____
_____

DATE: _____     HORSE: _____

## MY BIG GOAL
_____
_____

## TODAY I AM GRATEFUL FOR
01 _____
02 _____
03 _____

## TODAY'S EXERCISE & GOALS
01 _____
02 _____
03 _____

## ENERGY LEVEL OF HORSE (CIRCLE ONE)

## MY HORSE'S MOOD

## MY MOOD

## WEATHER

NOTES
_____
_____
_____
_____
_____
_____
_____
_____
_____
_____

# WEEK 2

## Progress Tracker

## SCORE

**What would you rate your QUALITY of performance over this exercise as a rider?** Rate Yourself!

(1 being abysmal, 10 being Bring on the Olympics!

| 1 | 2 | 3 | 4 | 5 | 6 | 7 | 8 | 9 | 10 |

**How was your rhythm, pace & adjustability or overall control of your horse during this exercise?** Rate Yourself!

| 1 | 2 | 3 | 4 | 5 | 6 | 7 | 8 | 9 | 10 |

**How was your accuracy & timing?** (Example: Were you able to get the movements on the exact letter.) Rate Yourself!

| 1 | 2 | 3 | 4 | 5 | 6 | 7 | 8 | 9 | 10 |

**How was your horse overall?** Rate Yourself!

| 1 | 2 | 3 | 4 | 5 | 6 | 7 | 8 | 9 | 10 |

**How was your ride overall?** Rate Yourself!

| 1 | 2 | 3 | 4 | 5 | 6 | 7 | 8 | 9 | 10 |

# WEEK 2
# AFTER WEEK REFLECTION
DOCUMENT YOUR PROGRESS!

WHAT HAS BEEN MY BIGGEST STRUGGLE SO FAR?

WHAT IS ONE UNEXPECTED DISCOVERY OR LIGHTBULB MOMENT I HAD THIS WEEK?

WHAT HAS BEEN MY BIGGEST WIN THIS WEEK?

HOW CAN I IMPROVE NEXT WEEK?

WHAT QUESTION COULD I ASK IN THE GROUP OR TO THE INTERNATIONAL EQUESTRIAN TEAM TO HELP ME ON MY QUEST?

# You Probably Want to Quit Right Now...

Congratulations on completing week 2 of the workbook!

Some of you feel like you are on FIRE! You feel like a total rockstar and you are pumped and excited to complete the rest of the exercises in this workbook.

But many of you might be feeling the opposite right about now. You might be feeling down, anxious, frustrated or even skeptical. Does this even work? Am I good enough? You might be thinking.

And that is why I wanted to schedule this very needed intermission to give you a BIG HUG and a word of encouragement.

**FACT:** Getting better sometimes feels like getting worse.
**FACT:** It's easier to quit and do nothing and stay the same, then it is to continue, improve and succeed. If it were easy, we'd all be in the Olympics.
**FACT:** Quitting won't help you follow your North Star & get you to your goal. If you don't quit, you cannot fail. The destination isn't what's important, but the journey is.

Before week 1 you were probably feeling pretty good about your riding skills because you've done similar exercises before, or similiar ones already. You just needed a few tips and ideas... but now you are more aware of what you are doing wrong and you are probably feeling worse than you did before.

That's normal!

It's called "Raising Your Standards" (show jumping joke!) and becoming a better rider.

Not being aware of your mistakes doesn't make you a better rider, it just makes you ignorant and blind. That is why there are millions of equestrians right now that will NEVER move up to higher levels. They like to blame their finances (oh if I could afford an imported horse from Germany) or the weather (oh if I could train all year round) or their age (I don't bounce like I used to!) when in fact the only reason 97% of people on this planet will never achieve their goals is because of one thing and one thing only...

They quit.

Most of them before they even try! They quit before they even start. That is why I wanted to congratulate you on reaching the half way point! You're already well ahead of the other 97 percenters!

Don't stop now!

Part of developing our eye is being able to see and feel when something is wrong. That way, when it's right you can go **AH HA!** That's what it feels like when it's right! How do I duplicate that feeling and get it more frequently?

That is most likely where you are right now in your training journey. Don't stop! Push through and WAX ON WAX OFF!

**Need extra support? Let's Talk!**
**https://www.theinternationalequestrian.com/freestrategycall**

# WEEK 2
# BONUS MINDSET /
# NON-RIDING EXERCISE

## Laughter is the Best Medicine

It's scientifically proven that our body remains in a relaxed state for up to 45 minutes after laughter. When we are relaxed, our horses are relaxed. Less falls occur, horses are happier, riders are happier... it's a win win situation for everyone!

That is why this week your homework is to watch at least 1 stand up comedian which is not making rude or negative jokes. It's important the comedian not be rude or negative because the point of this exercise is to laugh but also laugh in a posiitve way and bring positive energy and vibes to ourselves and our horses.

Some recommended comedians: Trevor Noah or Jim Gaffigan. Another good one is the British Comedian Michael McIntyre or the Irish Comedian Dara Ó Briain.

You can find them on YouTube, Netflix, Amazon and more.

Or spend 20 minutes watching funny cat videos. The point is, spend at least 1 hour this week LAUGHING!

Share on the next page: How did this exercise make you feel? Do you believe laughter and doing this exercise could help you build a stronger bond with your horse? How?

# WEEK 2
# MINDSET HOMEWORK

Complete your mindset homework assignment for this week using the blank page below.

# WEEK 3

**Your mission for week 3 is to become confident in your own power & unleash your inner glow.**

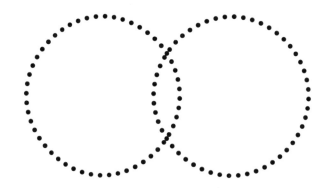

# Motivational Quotes to Pump You Up For Week 3!

"Be not afraid of going slowly. Be afraid only of standing still." – Chinese proverb

"Courage is being scared to death, but saddling up anyway." – John Wayne

"Twenty years from now you will be more disappointed by the things that you didn't do than by the ones you did do." – Mark Twain

"If you want to achieve excellence, you can get there today. As of this second, quit doing less-than-excellent work." – Thomas J. Watson

"It takes as much energy to wish as it does to plan." – Eleanor Roosevelt

"Opportunities don't happen. You create them." – Chris Grosser

"If you're going through hell, keep going." – Winston Churchill

"Don't be afraid to give up the good to go for the great." – John D. Rockefeller

"You must either modify your dreams or magnify your skills." – Jim Rohn

# Your Road Map to Success

## SECOND WEEK

- Re-programming muscle memory
- Finding your center & balance
- Establishing partnership with your horse
- Building horse & rider fitness

## FIRST WEEK

**1**

- Establishing your baseline
- Relaxing warmup stretches to loosen tightness, stiffness & tension.
- Establishing new routine
- Breaking it all down so we can rebuild you back up

**2**

**3**

## THIRD WEEK

- Spicing things up and adding a new layer of difficulty
- Establishing quality with more technical exercises
- Pushing you to be the best you can be

## FOURTH WEEK

**4**

- Test week
- "Show day" simulation training - putting it all together
- New habits, muscle memory and fitness kicks in
- Technical Riding

www.theinternationalequestrian.com

# WEEK 3
# WARMUP LESSON PLAN

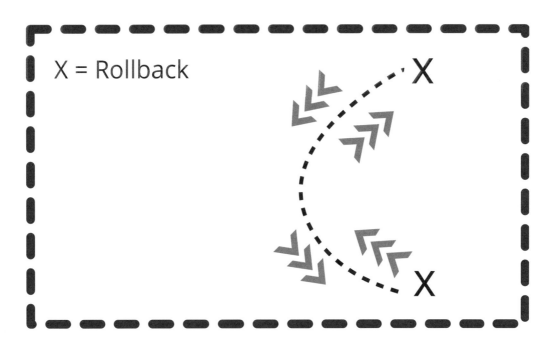

X = Rollback

## Half Moons

15 minutes

QUICK TIPS

**LISTEN TO OUR INTERACTIVE RIDE ALONG STORY "SHEEP HERDING IN GREENLAND" TO PUT THIS LESSON INTO ACTION!**

**Instructions:**

Spend the first 5 minutes allowing your horse to walk and trot (and possibly canter) on the buckle. Allow them to strech long and low. This will help them to lift their backs and warm them to prepare for the ride ahead. Next, gather your reins until you have a light and soft contact in your hands. If you are not taking advantage of the audio lessons inside our App, set a timer on your phone for 15 minutes.

First do the exercise in a walk, making sure to aim your horse not for the corner of the arena but the side of the wall. You want to halt your horse for the rollback turns a good distance away from the arena wall so you give your horse plenty of room to turn. Then once you've halted, use your outside rein, leg and seat bones to spin your horse on a dime 180 degrees. As you are still turning launch your horse forward into the walk and repeat on the other side of the arena in the opposite direction. (To make the half moon shape.)

Do this in walk and trot, remembering to sit deep in the saddle in the down transitions to really allow the horse to sit and slam on the brakes quickly. MAKE SURE YOUR HORSE IS WEARING BOOTS!

Once the timer has gone off you are finished! You can now move onto your main session exercise for the day.

**Benefits of this exercise:**
- Energizes your horse (great for lazy horses!)
- Focuses a hot horse & get's their ears on you
- Establishes your pre-flight check and gets the buttons working
- Gets your horse using their hindquarters and picks them up off the forehand.
- Helps improve their turns & rollbacks for future

# WEEK 3
# FIGURE-8 POLES

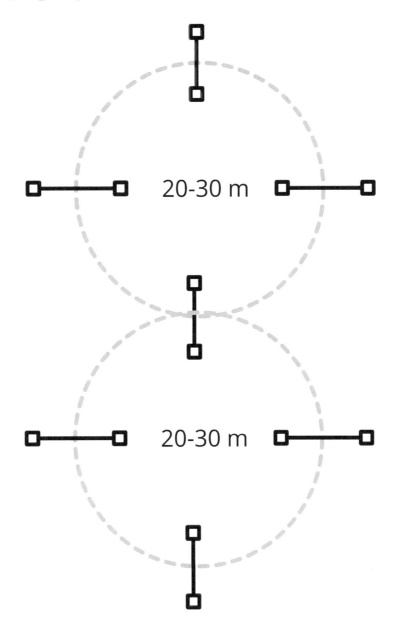

20-30 m

20-30 m

## Equipment Needed:

- 6 POLES
- 14 BLOCKS OR CAVALETTI

# WEEK 3
# VARIATIONS

## 1st Ride: Poles Only

Ride from both directions as poles on the ground. Try to count the same number of canter strides or trot steps between each pole, staying in the center of the poles.

## 2nd Ride: Raised Poles or Cavaletti

Gradually bump up the height of the poles using blocks, cavaletti or even cross rails. Approach from both directions and aim for the same number of strides between each pole.

## 3rd Ride: Varying Strides

For this ride you will try to vary your strides by shortening or lengthening your rhythm. Whether it be bigger trot steps and shorter trot steps or bigger or shorter canter strides. (Example: 5 Canter strides between each pole for a full Figure-8 loop followed by a Figure 8 loop of 4 canter strides and then 6 canter strides between each pole.)

**Helpful Tips:**

- Look with your eyes and heart.
- Stay sitting in the saddle for this exercise unless you make it a cross rail or jump later on. Then you can practice jumping seat over the poles.
- Experiment with making your circles bigger and smaller in order to adjust the strides without changing the rhythm of the horse.

**Common Mistakes:**

- Leaning into the circle. This will throw your horse off balance, making this exercise sloppy and messy. Sit tall, keep your horse balanced and back on their hinds. They should feel soft in your hands and go from the legs. They should feel active and springy. Make sure you achieve this feeling in your warmup before coming to your poles for your best chance of success.
- Looking down at your horse or the poles and not around the corner to the next pole. Plan your horses footsteps!
- Turning with the inside rein instead of the outside!

**Benefits of this Exercise:**

- This helps develop straightness and balance in your horse
- Rider coordination and accuracy as well as not leaning and turning with the outside rather than the inside rein

 **JUMPING IS DRESSAGE WITH OBSTACLES! WORK ON YOUR DRESSAGE BETWEEN THE JUMPS AND YOUR JUMPING WILL IMPROVE GREATLY!**

## Instructions:

This exercise is all about consistency of stride and keeping an even rhythm Also testing your ability to judge the path leading up to the pole in order to set your horse up for success and give them the same stride length.

Start this exercise in trot, simply keeping an even rhythm and showing them the poles and exercise. Count the steps out loud. You will also do this in canter!

Pick up the canter. You can choose to either pick up the lead which your horse is strongest to give them a positive first experience over the exercise, or you can choose to start with their worst lead to end on a good note when you change reins later.

Ride to the center of every pole, being careful not to make the path wider or shorter in different places of the circle. It has to be consistent! Count the strides, first riding the stride length which is comfortable for your horse--maybe 3 stides? 4 strides? Count! Then once you've completed a circle getting an even amount of strides over all 4 poles try adding a stride or taking a stride away. Repeat.

Ride over the exercise for at least 5-10 minutes on each side (taking regular walk breaks as needed.) You should maintain a nice rhythmical canter stride throughout the entire exercise.

In canter ask for your flying lead changes over the center pole but feel free to add variety so your horse doesn't anticipate the change by doing the same circle an extra lap before swapping to the other circle.

Give your horse a big pat and a scratch for a job well done!

# WEEK 3
# COOL DOWN LESSON PLAN

**Rising Walk**

Week 3 we start stepping things up a notch! This week is also focused on rider balance but we are cranking up the difficulty level. This week is designed to help your body undo all the years of bad muscle memory you have most likely programmed into your body, brain, nervous system and subconscious. We need to reset our systems and reprogram our brain's subconscious. That is the focus for this week.

**Instructions:**
Today's cool down exercise is for YOU, not your horse. Your horse need only trot with long loopy reins. They have the freedom to follow the rail mindlessly while you use this opportunity to focus on your own body and reprogramming your nervous system.

**How to do Rising Walk:**

Hold onto the saddle. You can hold onto a strap, the pommel or your horse's mane. You want to hold on and keep the reins long and loopy to ensure you don't accidentally bump your horse's mouth should you lose balance.

Next, start rising to the walk, just like you would rise to the trot. You should try to rise in the same rhythm as your horse's walk, but if you miss a few steps that is ok. Go at your own pace.

When rising, try to stand all the way up, really opening your hips and allowing your weight to sink into your lower legs and heels. When you sit in the saddle, do not fall into the saddle and drop heavily onto your horse's back. Try to sit gently onto your seat bones and then using your thigh muscles, core and abs to lift yourself straight into a standing position. You should only gently touch the saddle for a moment before rising again.

**Benefits of this exercise:**
- Stops knee gripping
- Activates and engages your thigh muscles
- Strengthens your thighs, abs and core
- Helps you use your muscles in order to rise rather than relying on the horse's motion to rise (something which happens in rising trot)
- Aids in having a more correct leg position by allowing your leg to relax and wrap around the belly of the horse.
- Improves rider balance, coordination and strength
- Helps the horse move more freely and have a happy mouth and back when the rider uses their own muscles for balance rather than their reins or dropping heavily onto their backs!

# BONUS
# CLASSROOM THEORY

Choose 1 Classroom Theory Video to watch this week. Use the blank space on the next page to take notes.

Interested vs Committed | Equestrian Motivation

The Difference Between Show Jumping in the USA vs Europe

1000 - Why is this number so crucial for equestrians with goals?

# WATCH FOR FREE ON OUR YOUTUBE CHANNEL!
## SUBSCRIBE TO GET NOTIFIED OF NEW VIDEO RELEASES.

Why you aren't at the riding level you want to be YET (5 steps to get...

The stunning 65 years young endurance rider who nearly sold h...

Break Your Bad Riding Habits FOR GOOD! (Horse Riding Lessons)

Building your dream team #equestrian #horse

3 Show Jumping Competition Tips For Amateur Hunter Jumpers

Time is Value. How to STOP Wasting Time & Level Up FASTER

 @coachkrystalkelly

# NOTES:

DATE: _____ HORSE: _____

MY BIG GOAL

_____

_____

TODAY I AM GRATEFUL FOR

01 _____

02 _____

03 _____

TODAY'S EXERCISE & GOALS

01 _____

02 _____

03 _____

## ENERGY LEVEL OF HORSE (CIRCLE ONE)

MY HORSE'S MOOD

MY MOOD

WEATHER

NOTES

_____

_____

_____

_____

_____

_____

_____

_____

_____

_____

# WEEK 3

## *Progress Tracker*

## SCORE

**What would you rate your QUALITY of performance over this exercise as a rider?** Rate Yourself!

(1 being abysmal, 10 being Bring on the Olympics!

| 1 | 2 | 3 | 4 | 5 | 6 | 7 | 8 | 9 | 10 |

**How was your rhythm, pace & adjustability or overall control of your horse during this exercise?** Rate Yourself!

| 1 | 2 | 3 | 4 | 5 | 6 | 7 | 8 | 9 | 10 |

**How was your accuracy & timing?** (Example: Were you able to get the movements on the exact letter.) Rate Yourself!

| 1 | 2 | 3 | 4 | 5 | 6 | 7 | 8 | 9 | 10 |

**How was your horse overall?** Rate Yourself!

| 1 | 2 | 3 | 4 | 5 | 6 | 7 | 8 | 9 | 10 |

**How was your ride overall?** Rate Yourself!

| 1 | 2 | 3 | 4 | 5 | 6 | 7 | 8 | 9 | 10 |

DATE: _____     HORSE: _____
_____

MY BIG GOAL
_____
_____

TODAY I AM GRATEFUL FOR
01 _____
02 _____
03 _____

TODAY'S EXERCISE & GOALS
01 _____
02 _____
03 _____

ENERGY LEVEL OF HORSE (CIRCLE ONE)

MY HORSE'S MOOD                    NOTES
☺ ☺ ☺ ☹ ☹ ☺ ☺         _____

MY MOOD                            _____
☺ ☺ ☺ ☹ ☹ ☺ ☺         _____

WEATHER                            _____
                                   _____
                                   _____
                                   _____
                                   _____
                                   _____
                                   _____

DATE: _____   HORSE: _____

## WEEK 3 NEW MUSCLE MEMORY RIDE #3

MY BIG GOAL
_____
_____

TODAY I AM GRATEFUL FOR
01 _____
02 _____
03 _____

TODAY'S EXERCISE & GOALS
_____
01 _____
02 _____
03 _____

ENERGY LEVEL OF HORSE (CIRCLE ONE)

MY HORSE'S MOOD

MY MOOD

WEATHER

NOTES
_____
_____
_____
_____
_____
_____
_____
_____
_____

www.THEINTERNATIONALEQUESTRIAN.com

# WEEK 3

## *Progress Tracker*

## SCORE

**What would you rate your QUALITY of performance over this exercise as a rider?** Rate Yourself!
(1 being abysmal, 10 being Bring on the Olympics!

| 1 | 2 | 3 | 4 | 5 | 6 | 7 | 8 | 9 | 10 |

**How was your rhythm, pace & adjustability or overall control of your horse during this exercise?** Rate Yourself!

| 1 | 2 | 3 | 4 | 5 | 6 | 7 | 8 | 9 | 10 |

**How was your accuracy & timing?** (Example: Were you able to get the movements on the exact letter.) Rate Yourself!

| 1 | 2 | 3 | 4 | 5 | 6 | 7 | 8 | 9 | 10 |

**How was your horse overall?** Rate Yourself!

| 1 | 2 | 3 | 4 | 5 | 6 | 7 | 8 | 9 | 10 |

**How was your ride overall?** Rate Yourself!

| 1 | 2 | 3 | 4 | 5 | 6 | 7 | 8 | 9 | 10 |

# WEEK 3
# AFTER WEEK REFLECTION
DOCUMENT YOUR PROGRESS!

WHAT HAS BEEN MY BIGGEST STRUGGLE SO FAR?

WHAT IS ONE UNEXPECTED DISCOVERY OR LIGHTBULB MOMENT I HAD THIS WEEK?

WHAT HAS BEEN MY BIGGEST WIN THIS WEEK?

HOW CAN I IMPROVE NEXT WEEK?

WHAT QUESTION COULD I ASK IN THE GROUP OR TO THE INTERNATIONAL EQUESTRIAN TEAM TO HELP ME ON MY QUEST?

# WEEK 4

**Your mission for week 4 is to challenge yourself, your horse & most importantly to laugh, smile & HAVE FUN!**

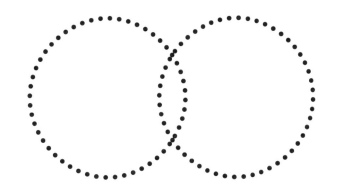

# Motivational Quotes to Pump You Up For Week 4!

"There's no fear when you're having fun." – Will Thomas

"Everyone wants to live on top of the mountain, but all the happiness and growth occurs while you're climbing it." – Andy Rooney

"Enjoy life. There's plenty of time to be dead." – Hans Christian Andersen

"The best way to pay for a lovely moment is to enjoy it." – Richard Bach

"If it's not fun, you're not doing it right." – Bob Basso

"There are going to be good times and bad times, but lighten up." – Chris Pine

"When you are not having fun, you're sort of missing the point." – Abraham

"We don't stop playing because we grow old; we grow old because we stop playing." – George Bernard Shaw

# Your Road Map to Success

## FIRST WEEK

- Establishing your baseline
- Relaxing warmup stretches to loosen tightness, stiffness & tension.
- Establishing new routine
- Breaking it all down so we can rebuild you back up

## SECOND WEEK

- Re-programming muscle memory
- Finding your center & balance
- Establishing partnership with your horse
- Building horse & rider fitness

**1**

**2**

**3**

**4**

## THIRD WEEK

- Spicing things up and adding a new layer of difficulty
- Establishing quality with more technical exercises
- Pushing you to be the best you can be

## FOURTH WEEK

- Test week
- "Show day" simulation training - putting it all together
- New habits, muscle memory and fitness kicks in
- Technical Riding

www.theinternationalequestrian.com

# WEEK 4
# WARMUP LESSON PLAN

**NEW RULE!**
No staying on the rail.
Bouncing off the rail only!
Creativity wins.

Be <u>unpredictable.</u>

## The Perfect Warm Up #6

15 minutes

QUICK TIPS

**IMPROVE YOUR ACCURACY BY SETTING SPECIFIC TARGETS. FOR EXAMPLE "I WILL MAKE A TRANSISTION AT EVERY DRESSAGE LETTER. OR MAYBE EVERY OTHER FENCE POST. GET CREATIVE AND TRY NOT TO BE "PREDICTABLE." KEEP YOUR HORSE'S EARS ON YOU THE ENTIRE WARM UP WITHOUT GETTING DISTRACTED AND YOU'LL KNOW YOU HAVE SUCCEEDED!**

**Instructions:**

Spend the first 5 minutes allowing your horse to walk and trot (and possibly canter) on the buckle. Allow them to strech long and low. This will help them to lift their backs and warm them to prepare for the ride ahead.

Today's exercise will be similar as previous Perfect Warm Ups you've done with us, but with one KEY difference.

You're not allowed to be on the rail! That's right today you are going to set a timer for 10-15 minutes and then you are going to do walk to halt, walk to trot, walk to canter transitions all while not being allowed to go on the rail. Rules: You may "bounce" off of the rail (touch the rail for a stride or two as in a circle) but you are not allowed to stay. That means lots of circles, diagonals, riding on the 3/4 line etc. All while incorporating different shortening and lengthening transitions as well as full transitions.

Make sure to change direction frequently! Your goal should be 100 transitions.

Once the timer has gone off you are finished! You can now move onto your main session exercise for the day.

**Benefits of this exercise:**
- Energizes your horse (great for lazy horses!)
- Helps hot horses to stay focused and relaxed (by keeping them busy they feel more at peace. That's because a bored horse is a naughty horse!)
- Establishes your pre-flight check and gets the buttons working
- Keeps things interesting and fun for horse and rider
- Gets the rider used to thinking on the fly and being spontaneous and fun

# WEEK 4
# DRESSAGE TEST

**How Your Test Will Work:**

The test you are about to complete inside this workbook is NOT a dressage test which can be found via the FEI, BHS or USDF. These are UNIQUE tests which we have designed based on the outcome you are trying to achieve over the last 4 weeks. *Note: Any similarities to a federation dressage test are purely coincidental.

Your test for this week will include movements which you have been working on during the last 4 weeks (and maybe a few new things sprinkled in just for fun.)

"But Coach Krystal, WHY?!" You ask. The answer is simple. Dressage is a French word meaning TRAINING. It does NOT mean turn right at C or Halt at X. The purpose behind dressage tests are to:

- Test the rider's accuracy and precision. Being able to perform an exact movement at an exact letter gives riders and judges a means of determining your level of accuracy.
- Challenge the horse and rider under pressure. It's one thing to do fancy dressage when no one is watching to your favorite Elvis Presley song ("You ain't nothin but a hound dog!"), it's another thing entirely to perform specific

movements at the specific moment you ask... for POINTS.

**How this test will work:**
You have three options.

1. Ride your tests and grade yourself based on how you think you did (you will fill out your scores using our dressage test sheet found on the following pages.)
2. Ask a friend or your instructor to judge you.
3. Let us judge your test for you!

If you are interested in letting our team of growing professionals judge your test, please purchase our "Virtual Dressage Test Show Critique" available on our store. This is a unique way of getting feedback and a score turned into you without having to trailer your horse to a show. If you live in a remote area with no professional coaches nearby, this is a great option and a fun way to check your progress.

If you use our Virtual Dressage Test Show Critique service you will get your test back including your score and feedback on how to improve / what to work on so you can make rapid progress. Then, when you are ready, feel free to sign up again and turn in your newly recorded video of you doing the test so our team can once again give you a graded test and video critique to help you on your journey!

However you choose to do your test, enjoy the journey and

remember to LAUGH, SMILE and HAVE FUN!

To sign up for our Virtual Dressage Test Show Video Critique please visit our website:

**https://coachkrystalkellybooks.com**

Scan Me

# WEEK 4
# DRESSAGE TEST

Rate Yourself!
1-10 (10 being Perfect)

| Instructions | 1st Ride | 2nd Ride | 3rd Ride |
|---|---|---|---|
| Enter at A, Halt Salute at X. | | | |
| Turn on haunches 180 degrees. Medium Walk. | | | |
| Halt at D. Turn on haunches 180 degrees opposite side. | | | |
| Working Trot to C track left. E 20 meter circle. | | | |
| F-X-H Extended or Lenthening Trot. H shorten trot. C turn down Centerline | | | |
| X halt. Turn on forehand 180 degrees. Medium walk. | | | |
| G Halt. Turn on forehand opposite side. Free walk | | | |
| L Pick up reins medium walk | | | |

| Instructions | 1st Ride | 2nd Ride | 3rd Ride |
|---|---|---|---|
| Track left at A. Working trot at F. B 20 meter circle. | | | |
| M halt. Left lead canter. 20 meter circle at C. | | | |
| E-X-B Flying or simple change at X. Track Right at B. | | | |
| 20 meter circle right lead canter at A. | | | |
| H working trot. C centerline. X halt salute. | | | |

| | | | |
|---|---|---|---|
| Total Points: | | | |
| Total Percentages: | | | |

To Get Your Total Score: Calculate the percentage of all your points by dividing your total points by the total marks possible for that test and multiplying by 100.

# WEEK 4
# RULES

## 1st Ride: Keep it Simple

For the first test focus on memorizing your test and practicing the movements. You don't have to do the full test without interruptions. Use this test as a chance to turn around and practice the same movement once or twice before moving on and continuing your test.

## 2nd Ride: Work Out the Kinks

In your warmup, focus on really practicing those movements you find the most challenging. Practice several times and then enter and do your test in full without interuptions.

## 3rd Ride: Show Day!

Submit your test to our Virtual Dressage Test Show Video Critique or treat it as if it were a real competition. Dress nice, braid your horse's mane, use some mane and tail detangler and make a day of it! Make it a special occasion and treat your test as if you are having a judge watch you. Invite your friends and family to watch or video yourself to submit your entry to our Virtual Dressage Test Show Video Critique! Most importantly, have fun!

# WEEK 4
# DRESSAGE TEST

**Helpful Tips:**

- Do not skip the show day! Having a day where you feel good about yourself and simply show off how amazing you and your horse are (with a bit of adrenaline and pressure!) is a great way to really put yourself to the test.
- It's important to work out all the kinks before your show day. That way you can go slow, take your time to focus on the turns or any challenges you may face later. Fix them in your first and second session. Show day isn't the time to fix your mistakes. Training day is! Today is the time to train.

**Benefits of this Exercise:**

- Practicing dressage tests helps us to put all the pieces together, figure out what's missing and what we need to improve or work on and allows us the opportunity to challenge our horses and selves in a quick, adrenaline inducing environment. This environment tests us and helps shine a light on what there is to improve and also shines a light on what is working well and how much of a team mate and partner you are with your horse. It also helps you to improve your timing and accuracy.

 **QUICK TIPS**

**SMILE! SMILING CAN HELP US FEEL MORE CONFIDENT AND HELPS US HAVE FUN WITH OUR HORSES. REMEMBER, HAVING FUN IS WHAT THIS IS ALL ABOUT FOR BOTH US AND OUR HORSES SO IF YOU AREN'T HAVING FUN YOUR HORSE WON'T HAVE FUN EITHER!**

# WEEK 4
# DRAW YOUR TEST

Use the blank pages to draw out your test. VISUALIZE IT!

# WEEK 4
# DRAW YOUR TEST
Use the blank pages to draw out your test. VISUALIZE IT!

# WEEK 4
# COOL DOWN LESSON PLAN

**Hips, Airplane, Sky in Canter**

Week 4 we are stepping on the gas even more! This week is also focused on rider balance but we are cranking up the difficulty level. This week is designed to help your body undo all the years of bad muscle memory you have most likely programmed into your body, brain, nervous system and subconscious. We need to reset our systems and reprogram our brain's subconscious. That is the focus for this week.

**Instructions:**
Today's cool down exercise is for YOU, not your horse. Your horse need only canter with long loopy reins. They have the freedom to follow the rail mindlessly while you use this opportunity to focus on your own body and reprogramming your nervous system.

**How to do Hips, Airplane, Sky in Canter:**

Place your reins somewhere where they won't slip down (tuck it over your half pad or hold the reins loosely with one hand, swapping hands as you do the exercise.)

Ask your horse for a steady canter following the rail. Then place your hands on your hips. Let them rest there for a step or two before stretching both arms out wide to the side and let them pull in opposite directions as if someone is trying to make your arms longer. Lastly, reach your arms high in the sky, again feeling as if you are being pulled upwards with your entire body (while keeping your seat in the saddle.) Repeat as many times as needed for at least one lap each direction.

Enjoy the stretches! Allow your body to relax and move with the natural movements of your horse without interfering or trying to lock your joints or brace. Remember to BREATHE. This is your chance to stretch, relax and center yourself.

**Benefits of this exercise:**
- Opens shoulders
- Stretches your back, shoulders and neck
- Deepens seat
- Connects rider with horse
- Strengthens core
- Relaxes your muscles and body
- Allows you the opportunity to move freely with your horse without resistance or bracing
- Burns belly fat
- Fights stress
- Improves your balance and coordination

DATE: _____     HORSE: _____

## MY BIG GOAL
_____
_____

## TODAY I AM GRATEFUL FOR
01 _____
02 _____
03 _____

## TODAY'S EXERCISE & GOALS
01 _____
02 _____
03 _____

### ENERGY LEVEL OF HORSE (CIRCLE ONE)

MY HORSE'S MOOD

MY MOOD

WEATHER

NOTES
_____
_____
_____
_____
_____
_____
_____
_____
_____

**WEEK 4 BASELINE RIDE #1**

# WEEK 4

## Progress Tracker

## SCORE

**What would you rate your QUALITY of performance over this exercise as a rider?** Rate Yourself!
(1 being abysmal, 10 being Bring on the Olympics!

| 1 | 2 | 3 | 4 | 5 | 6 | 7 | 8 | 9 | 10 |

**How was your rhythm, pace & adjustability or overall control of your horse during this exercise?** Rate Yourself!

| 1 | 2 | 3 | 4 | 5 | 6 | 7 | 8 | 9 | 10 |

**How was your accuracy & timing?** (Example: Were you able to get the movements on the exact letter.) Rate Yourself!

| 1 | 2 | 3 | 4 | 5 | 6 | 7 | 8 | 9 | 10 |

**How was your horse overall?** Rate Yourself!

| 1 | 2 | 3 | 4 | 5 | 6 | 7 | 8 | 9 | 10 |

**How was your ride overall?** Rate Yourself!

| 1 | 2 | 3 | 4 | 5 | 6 | 7 | 8 | 9 | 10 |

DATE: _____  HORSE: _____

MY BIG GOAL

_____

_____

TODAY I AM GRATEFUL FOR

01 _____

02 _____

03 _____

TODAY'S EXERCISE & GOALS

01 _____

02 _____

03 _____

### ENERGY LEVEL OF HORSE (CIRCLE ONE)

MY HORSE'S MOOD

NOTES

MY MOOD

WEATHER

_____

DATE: _____          HORSE: _____

# WEEK 4 NEW MUSCLE MEMORY RIDE #3

MY BIG GOAL
_____
_____

TODAY I AM GRATEFUL FOR
01 _____
02 _____
03 _____

TODAY'S EXERCISE & GOALS
_____
01 _____
02 _____
03 _____

ENERGY LEVEL OF HORSE (CIRCLE ONE)

MY HORSE'S MOOD

MY MOOD

WEATHER

NOTES
_____
_____
_____
_____
_____
_____
_____
_____

# WEEK 4

## *Progress Tracker*

## SCORE

**What would you rate your QUALITY of performance over this exercise as a rider?** Rate Yourself!

(1 being abysmal, 10 being Bring on the Olympics!

| 1 | 2 | 3 | 4 | 5 | 6 | 7 | 8 | 9 | 10 |
|---|---|---|---|---|---|---|---|---|----|

**How was your rhythm, pace & adjustability or overall control of your horse during this exercise?** Rate Yourself!

| 1 | 2 | 3 | 4 | 5 | 6 | 7 | 8 | 9 | 10 |
|---|---|---|---|---|---|---|---|---|----|

**How was your accuracy & timing?** (Example: Were you able to get the movements on the exact letter.) Rate Yourself!

| 1 | 2 | 3 | 4 | 5 | 6 | 7 | 8 | 9 | 10 |
|---|---|---|---|---|---|---|---|---|----|

**How was your horse overall?** Rate Yourself!

| 1 | 2 | 3 | 4 | 5 | 6 | 7 | 8 | 9 | 10 |
|---|---|---|---|---|---|---|---|---|----|

**How was your ride overall?** Rate Yourself!

| 1 | 2 | 3 | 4 | 5 | 6 | 7 | 8 | 9 | 10 |
|---|---|---|---|---|---|---|---|---|----|

# WEEK 4
# AFTER WEEK REFLECTION
DOCUMENT YOUR PROGRESS!

WHAT HAS BEEN MY  BIGGEST STRUGGLE SO FAR?

WHAT IS ONE UNEXPECTED DISCOVERY OR LIGHTBULB MOMENT I HAD THIS WEEK?

WHAT HAS BEEN MY BIGGEST WIN THIS WEEK?

HOW CAN I IMPROVE NEXT WEEK?

WHAT QUESTION COULD I ASK IN THE GROUP OR TO THE INTERNATIONAL EQUESTRIAN TEAM TO HELP ME ON MY QUEST?

# CONGRATS!

**You have completed your quest! What's next?**

# END OF WORKBOOK
# REFLECTION
DOCUMENT YOUR PROGRESS!

WHAT IS ONE UNEXPECTED DISCOVERY OR LIGHTBULB MOMENT I HAD DURING THIS PROCESS?

WHAT HAVE BEEN SOME OF MY BIGGEST IMPROVEMENTS THROUGHOUT THIS EXPERIENCE?

WHAT HAS BEEN MY BIGGEST WIN?

WHAT IMPROVEMENTS HAVE I FELT IN MY HORSE?

WHAT WOULD I LIKE TO WORK ON OR IMPROVE FOR THE NEXT 30 DAYS? (SEE OUR LIST OF OTHER WORKBOOKS IN OUR SERIES AT THE END OF THE BOOK TO HELP YOU DECIDE!)

HOW CAN I KEEP THIS MOMENTUM GOING FORWARD?

# Circles & Corners
# "After" Self-Assessment

At the beginning of this workbook you filled out your "Before" Self-Assessment. Please rate yourself below and then compare your "Before" & "After!" Share your results inside our Facebook Group and make sure you pop a bottle of bubbly or take your family out to eat to celebrate your amazing success!

**Do you consistently & accurately ride corners and circles?** Rate Yourself! (1 being almost never, 10 being Bring on the Olympics!)

| 1 | 2 | 3 | 4 | 5 | 6 | 7 | 8 | 9 | 10 |
|---|---|---|---|---|---|---|---|---|---|

**How often would you say your horse leans on circles and turns or falls in or out in turns?** Rate Yourself! (1 being frequently, 10 being never.)

| 1 | 2 | 3 | 4 | 5 | 6 | 7 | 8 | 9 | 10 |
|---|---|---|---|---|---|---|---|---|---|

**How is your position and balance?** (Example: Do you fall behind the motion of the horse or struggle in canter?) Rate Yourself!

| 1 | 2 | 3 | 4 | 5 | 6 | 7 | 8 | 9 | 10 |
|---|---|---|---|---|---|---|---|---|---|

**How often do you and your horse "argue?"** Rate Yourself!

| 1 | 2 | 3 | 4 | 5 | 6 | 7 | 8 | 9 | 10 |
|---|---|---|---|---|---|---|---|---|---|

**How would you rate your overall riding ability?** Rate Yourself!

| 1 | 2 | 3 | 4 | 5 | 6 | 7 | 8 | 9 | 10 |
|---|---|---|---|---|---|---|---|---|---|

# Congratulations! You Did it!

Wow! What an amazing accomplishment you have just achieved. So many people start things they never finish. But that's not you! You signed a contract to yourself at the beginning of this workbook and you kept your word and promise to yourself. For that alone you should be proud.

Now it's time to celebrate! Make sure you pop a bottle of bubbly, take your family out for a date night or schedule a nice weekend getaway somewhere fun. You deserve it!

If you enjoyed this workbook and are ready to keep the momentum going please check out our other workbooks on Amazon and select your next 28 day challenge.

As a reward for your hard work, enjoy 15% on your next purchase on our website. Use code: **15forme at checkout.**

**https://coachkrystalkellybooks.com/**

Wishing you many more years of fun and adventures with your horse!

Much Love,

Scan Me

Dear reader,

We hope you've enjoyed your journey with us. We are on a mission to raise the standards in the equestrian sports and create millions of world class horse riders around the globe. To help us with our mission, please consider leaving us a positive review on Amazon.

This review might seem like a simple act but it helps immensely by letting other horse lovers like you find our workbooks in order to apply these strategies to their own riding routines. We greatly appreciate your kind reviews and can't wait to hear how much you enjoyed the ride!

Share your photos and videos on our website with your testimonial for 15-20% off your next purchase!

**https://coachkrystalkellybooks.com/**

-The TIE Team

# Other Helpful Show Jumping & Dressage Guide To Workbooks To Assist You On Your Journey

- Seeing Strides
- Verticals
- Oxers
- Courses
- Combinations
- Bending Lines
- Building Top line
- Control Between Fences
- Rider Position
- Rider Balance
- A Sticky Butt
- Confidence
- Conquering Fear
- Competitions
- Competing Internationally
- Jump Offs
- A Steady Leg
- Soft Hands
- Jumping Dressage
- Success Mindset
- Rollbacks & Tight Turns
- Spooky Jumps
- Green Horse's First Course
- Jumping Bigger
- Developing your "Eye"
- Clear Rounds

- Perfecting Rhythm
- Circles and Corners
- Rider Position
- Building Topline
- Mastering Contact
- A Sticky Butt
- Rider Confidence
- Success Mindset
- Mastering Impulsion
- Mastering Straightness

**Order your next workbook on Amazon today!**

# Other Books By Krystal Kelly

- **The Ambitious Equestrian:** How to Implement the Secrets of Grand Prix Riders to Achieve Your Wildest Goals. (In Your Free Time.)
- **The 90 Day Horse Riding Training Journal**
- **Saddles and Sisterhood:** Equestrian Adventuresses Series Book 1
- **Going the Distance:** Equestrian Adventuresses Series Book 2
- **Leg Up:** Equestrian Adventuresses Series Book 3
- **Have Breeches Will Travel:** Equestrian Adventuresses Series Book 4
- **Horse Nomads:** Equestrian Adventuresses Series Book 5
- **Around the World on 180 Horses** (Book 1: The Quest for Dracula's Lost Treasure)
- **Around the World on 180 Horses** (Book 2: The Quest for the Hidden Viking Hoard)
- **10 Minute Easy Eye Yoga:** Improve Your Eyesight Naturally
- **Speaking the Horse Language:** How to unlock the hidden messages we send our horses in order to build an unshakable bond.
- **How to Work and Volunteer Abroad with Horses**
- **Horse Riding in Every Country**
- **Horse Riding Travel Guide Books** (6 Books Series)

**Order your copy on Amazon or Audible today!**

# Your Roadmap to Success

**YOU ARE HERE**

**6 Months**

**3 Months**

**9 Months**

**12 Months**

### 3 Months
- Rebuild correct foundation
- Re-Install Correct Position, Balance & Muscle Memory using targeted exercises focusing on biomechanics
- NO JUMPING!
- Phase one: RIDER
- Build strong bond
- Ask about our Sticky Butt Bootcamp

### 6 Months
- Leveraging Key Pole Exercises to install the correct Foundation for your horse.
- Begin mixing targeted jumping exercises to prepare you for more technical courses and jumps.
- Ask about our Polework Intensive

### 9 Months
- Pre-Competition Training, introducing more complex and challeng jumping exercises to prepare horse and rider for courses and shows
- Enter in schooling shows

### 12 Months
- Competition Time!
- Enter in various shows, tweak, improve.

## HAVE YOU ENJOYED TRAINING WITH US? WOULD YOU LIKE TO CONTINUE?

## ASK US ABOUT OUR STICKY BUTT BOOTCAMP, OUR POLEWORK INSTENSIVE OR OUR 3, 6 OR 12 MONTH COACHING NEXT!

info@theinternationalequestrian.com

# *Client*
# TESTIMONIALS

The International Equestrian™ VIP Inner Circle

**Kim**
2h · ☺

Just got back from my fifth Competive trail ride with Victor. He continues to improve each ride! I'm pleased with our progress. This ride was held on a ranch in Valley Mills, Texas that is beautiful but with very technical and challenging terrain. It was rocky with steep inclines and had deep ravines filled with water and beautiful fields with abundant fragrant bluebonnets. My key take away this week is to "stop and settle" before and during obstacles as necessary. We went too fast backing through an L shaped obstacle and stepped out of bounds. So I need to take one step at a time and breathe to help relax Victor and myself. On a very positive note our trot outs are now amazing! Y'all, I feel like my brain is actually re-wiring itself! I'm actually having fun and learning instead of being negative and critical of my performance. It's all good and getting better with a change in attitude! ☺

"You can only get better on this program. Wish I'd had this program 40 years ago. Just do it!" ●●●
- 75 year old Gail from New Zealand

**Gina**
Top contributor  Just now · 🌐

Hi everyone. I'm starting to get in a routine. Feeling more confident even in baby stages. This is because I finally have a plan, guidance, and understand the science of things. So even though I am still struggling in the sticky stage, I feel I can do it for once and not just be a spectator and wish away that I could be a good equestrian. I feel pride in what im doing now. I like I have a coach like Krystal . I feel like she is my professor keeping me accountable for my classes to pass and keep organized like in grad school.

Thanks everyone!

**The International Equestrian Sticky Butt™ Bootcamp Mastermind**   ···   ✕
Kim

I haven't posted in awhile- it's been crazy busy. I'm SO glad I found Krystal Kelly and this group. I ride english and was talked into western by good friends who helped with tack & equipment. We had our first show last weekend and we did great! We won command class (which is basically Simon says–3 strides to get the gait, plus halts, turn on haunches, extending gaits etc). We do the perfect warm up so often that my horse is fabulous at transitions!! We did the audio stories on the trail to practice our sitting trot (rode with some gauchos! LOL!). We placed second in trail class and did ok in pleasure and equitation. We also had a clean sweep the day before in our English classes! I can't say enough how much the audio lessons and sticky butt training has helped! We are having so much fun and I'm so happy to be showing again after a 30 year hiatus.

https://www.theinternationalequestrian.com/sticky-butt-bootcamp

SCAN ME

🎓 **Claim your** 🎓
## $500 Scholarship

As a thank you for getting my book... I'd like to extend you a very special invitation for a select few lucky riders to join me for our "Sticky Butt Bootcamp" Coaching. These lucky riders will recieve a $500 scholarship to apply on their tuition fees.

All you have to do is visit our website. If we have openings please use this special code: **stickybuttersunite500** at checkout to enroll and save **$500 on your tuition fees.**

*Limited availability: If there are no openings you can get on our waitlist by emailing us at: info@theinternationalequestrian.com

# Her investment into our 1 Year Virtual Coaching Program with The International Equestrian Got Her Amazing Results!

## Kim

Endurance Rider from Texas

"

I love sending in the videos to Coach Krystal, watching myself improve with the videos is something you just can't get in a normal lesson.

## Watch Kim's Interview

*Before*

- I was going to have to sell my horse because it was just a bad situation and I realized I wasn't going to be able to ride him safely or confidently.
- Paying for expensive dressage lessons and hauling my horse to a trainer wasn't helping. I felt like I wasn't learning and my relationship with my horse was going nowhere.
- I wasn't confident to train him myself.
- I was nervous, and definitely more of a follower than a leader. I wasn't able to be the leader my horse needed me to be.

*After*

- I have so much confidence now and I know how to handle him if he throws a few bucks on an endurance ride or gets excited.
- I ranked first for the entire NATRC competitions in my division even though my horse is green & it was both our first time doing these classes!
- I KNOW I'm a good rider now and we can do anything together that we set our minds too.
- I'm able to ride my horse confidently solo or with others in new places and trickier trails. He can even lead the other horses across water and bridges.
- My horse and I are partners now and have a strong relationship. I have even been "roping" off of him and dragging things behind him with a rope!
- I'm no longer a follower but a confident leader & team mate for my 4-legged friend.

https://www.theinternationalequestrian.com/freestrategycall

# *About* COACH KRYSTAL KELLY

Coach Krystal Kelly began working with horses in 2005 in California where she grew up. She pursued her passion for show jumping relentlessly, eventually going to an equestrian school for 2 years before graduating top of her class and moving onto a second equestrian College on the East Coast at the age of 19. During her time at the equestrian college she collected a number of certifications before stepping into the international ring, leaving the USA to pursue a career as a show jumper in Europe, Africa, Asia and the Middle East.

Working almost exclusively with Grand Prix Show Jumping horses she pursued her FEI II Coaching Certification which she received in Greece in 2016. She began developing her own riding curriculum wanting to impact and help others succeed in the sport. Coach Krystal is the CEO of The International Equestrian LLC, successfully empowering equestrians around the globe to get the training and education that is lacking in the industry, and has helped tens of thousands of clients in over 146 countries over the past 19 years.

When she's not coaching riders to achieve their dreams, Krystal enjoys riding her own horses where she lives in Spain at her own private show jumping stable. She loves going for hikes with her dogs, traveling and learning about new cultures and languages.

Above all, Coach Krystal believes that the relationship you build with your horse should come first and that reaching for Grand Prix dreams should be a skillset you use to improve the lives of those you love most. That includes being a role model to other fellow equestrians and helping to raise the standards of equestrian education around the globe. She is also a firm believer that women can ride just as good as men, no matter how male dominated it get's the further you climb to the top of the pyramid. She promotes more women Grand Prix riders and hopes to see women out numbering men at the top!

Inquiries for podcast appearances, film, workshops, clinics or speaking events can be sent to: info@theinternationalequestrian.com.

# NOTES:

# NOTES:

# NOTES:

# NOTES:

# NOTES:

# NOTES:

Made in United States
Troutdale, OR
12/07/2024

26053006R00091